A SPIRITED HISTORY OF
MILWAUKEE
BREWS & BOOZE

A SPIRITED HISTORY OF
MILWAUKEE
BREWS&BOOZE

MARTIN HINTZ

THE
History
PRESS

Published by The History Press
Charleston, SC 29403
www.historypress.net

Copyright © 2011 by Martin Hintz
All rights reserved
Front cover: Courtesy of Nancy Moore Gettelman.
Back cover, upper left and middle: Courtesy of Miller Coors-Milwaukee.
Lower left: Courtesy of Sensient Technologies.

First published 2011
Manufactured in the United States

ISBN 978.1.60949.066.9

Library of Congress Cataloging-in-Publication Data

Hintz, Martin.
A spirited history of Milwaukee brews and booze / Martin Hintz.
p. cm.
ISBN 978-1-60949-066-9
1. Brewing industry--Wisconsin--Milwaukee--History. 2. Breweries--Wisconsin--
Milwaukee--History. 3. Distilleries--Wisconsin--Milwaukee--History. I. Title.
HD9397.U53M554 2011
338.4'7663420977595--dc23
2011020343

Contents

The First Pour

I'll have another, please.
—Delegate, Moonshiners Convention of Bald Headed Men, Neumueller's Park,
June 30, 1889[1]

Historically speaking, the first chapter of Wisconsin's brewing and distilling industries in Wisconsin actually began with the French. Etienne Brule is credited with having reached northern Wisconsin in the 1620s during his explorations of Lake Superior, and he probably had a bottle or two of cognac stashed in his canoe. Following Jean Nicolet's landing near Green Bay in 1634, French merchants sought beaver skins from the territory's Native Americans, exchanging metal knives, kettles, steel flints, guns and ammunition, woolen blankets and other goods for the valuable pelts. Alcohol, however, was officially prohibited but still easily obtained. All these trade goods were shipped though Mackinac at the head of Lake Michigan and then on to posts in Green Bay, Prairie du Chien and LaPointe.[2]

Over the next generations, most new colonists departed Europe in early March for the six- to eight-week ocean voyage to Canada or New York. From there, the typical immigrant traveled by boat up the St. Lawrence or Hudson Rivers, often through Albany and on to the Erie Canal, across Lake Erie and sailing to Lake Michigan ports such as Milwaukee. Others landed in New Orleans and came up the Mississippi River. The extended journey was enough for a traveler to work up a good thirst. Once settled, the newcomers went to work. For farmers, hops were among the first crops planted in frontier Wisconsin. The hardy vine was common in settler gardens, being used for animal fodder, human consumption, making dye, basket weaving and a multitude of other purposes—such as brewing beer.[3]

James Weaver is credited with being one of the first growers to bring hop roots to the frontier of southern Wisconsin in 1837. He raised the plant on his farm in Sussex, near Milwaukee. A native of Peasmarsh, Sussex County, England, Weaver had lived in New York State, where he grew hops prior to coming to Wisconsin. Also in the spring of 1837, Weaver's brother-in-law, David Bonham, opened a small "public house," making his own malt beverages in small batches. Since Weaver's crops had not yet been harvested, Bonham most likely used English or Eastern hops, which he probably purchased from lake freighters at harbor in Milwaukee.[4]

The 1840s saw the advent of the beer business in the burgeoning village of Milwaukee, since it was the beverage of choice preferred by the growing numbers of immigrants. While their Yankee neighbors drank whiskey, the latest arrivals—or at least the Germans—gathered in their neighborhood taverns. They'd sit around the stammtisch, the "table of regulars," to drink beer and discuss the latest news. Of course, it helped that the savviest saloonkeepers laid out a goodly supply of free *blutwurst* (blood sausage), pickled pigs' feet, headcheese and slabs of rye bread to go along with the froth.[5]

According to early newspapers, Welsh natives Owens, Pawlett and Davis erected the city's first brewery on the south side of the foot of Huron Street in the spring of 1840. The men opened their Lake Brewery, a small frame building that "furnished a sufficient quantity of ale and beer to quench the thirst of all lovers of malt liquor in Eastern Wisconsin. In 1845, the proprietors were obliged to enlarge the premises and during the past year a large brick addition has been built. Richard Owens, Esq., one of the original owners is now sole proprietor, the lesser being Messrs. Powell & Co."[6]

The second brewery in the city was opened in 1841 by German émigré Hermann Reuthlisberger (or Reutelshofer), located at the corner of Hanover and Virginia Streets (now South Third and West Virginia) in Walker's Point. Reuthlisberger's brew was popular, but he was underfinanced, soon selling his operations to baker John B. Meyer. In 1844, Meyer unloaded the business to his father-in-law, Francis Neukirch, who carried on the brewery under the Neukirch name. After the Lake Brewery opening, Levi Blossom started his Eagle Brewery, a finely appointed establishment tucked under a hill south of Chestnut Street. About that time, young Phillip Best launched another beer-making operation in the same neighborhood.[7]

The First Pour

In 1849, Wisconsin hosted 22 breweries. By 1856, Milwaukee alone had 20 breweries. In 1859, the number of beer manufacturers across the state had risen to 166. By 1860, nearly 200 breweries operated in Wisconsin, with more than 40 in Milwaukee, although most were quite small. But who cared about size as long as they made beer? Almost every town had a brewery, and some towns formed around breweries.[8] Milwaukee was certainly a place where the phrase "roll out the barrel" was taken seriously.

2

The Beer Barons

No man should drink too much beer, even if it was good beer, and that forty or fifty glasses a day ought to be the limit for anybody.
—Captain Frederick Pabst[1]

Milwaukee's entrepreneurial families were closely connected from the city's earliest days. As with medieval fiefdoms in the Old Country, the star players in the community's upscale world married within their social and economic strata, as did their sons and daughters and, ultimately, many of their grandchildren. Thus did the dynasties thrive and survive. Uihleins were linked with the Pabsts, Brumders, Pfisters, Falks, Vogels, Mitchells, Isleys and others who lived wealthy lives in the New World. Many brewers married the widows of other brewers or the daughter of the boss. Marrying for love was great, but it helped if there was a beer keg in there somewhere, too.[2]

Much like a family, despite intermarriage and even close personal friendships, Milwaukee's brewers were often an argumentative bunch. To help resolve issues, they formed the Milwaukee Brewers Association to discuss matters of joint concern, from labor issues to pricing. The barons met regularly at the Second Ward Savings Bank, nicknamed the "Brewers' Bank," where dues were in relationship to the size of the brewery.

In addition to lobbying against such forces as the growing temperance movement, the loose-knit association also emphasized philanthropy.

Over the years, Milwaukee's brewing industry ebbed and flowed due to economy of scale and drinkers' tastes. The numbers of breweries declined, mostly due to buyouts and consolidation: from sixteen in 1879 to fourteen in 1890, to twelve in 1910, to eleven in 1935, to six in 1950 and to only three in 1973.[3] Now, the majority of the most fabled corporate names from history are merely produced on a contract basis with another brewery, a conglomerate often not even in Milwaukee.

Yet the following are among the many that have remained in the city's collective historical memory, its architecture, its ethos and its folklore.

Jos. Schlitz Brewing Company

The Schlitz beer story is not only that of the Schlitz brand but also about the larger-than-life personalities who managed the brewery for more than a century.

The story begins in Miltenberg, a Bavarian town along the Main River, now a large industrial city with two regional breweries: Kalt-Loch-Bräu and Brauhaus Faust. Miltenberg's local attractions include the remains of two Roman forts, built about AD 155. In addition to a couple archbishops and assorted dukes, one of its most noted native sons was Georg August Krug.[4] Krug emigrated from Miltenberg in 1848 with a wave of other émigrés from the assorted petty states and fiefdoms then composing Germany. Remaining behind in the Old Country, Krug's sister, Katherine, and her husband, Benedikt Uihlein, operated a gasthaus called Zur Krone (The Crown). Eventually settling in Milwaukee, one of the most Germanic of America's cities, Krug opened a restaurant in the Kilbourntown neighborhood in 1849. Ever frugal, Krug figured "why buy beer" when he could brew it. Hampered by the lack of refrigeration, he was still able to produce 250 barrels of beer in his basement during his first year.[5]

August Krug, Georg August's father, decided to visit his son in 1850, carrying a stash of $800 in gold to help the young man expand his operations in America. Accompanying the elder Krug was Katherine and Benedikt's eldest son, August Uihlein, then only eight years old. The two survived a shipwreck, saving themselves and—luckily for future beer drinkers worldwide—the money.[6]

Little August Uihlein was enrolled in Milwaukee's German-English Academy and then attended St. Louis University in Missouri between 1855 and 1857. Finishing school, he became a messenger boy for the Second Ward Bank and was later sent back to Missouri to learn the beer trade, becoming a bookkeeper in St. Louis's Uhrig Brewery.[7]

His grandfather's cash was put to good use once safely deposited in Milwaukee. The money enabled his uncle to hire Joseph Schlitz, a twenty-year-old bookkeeper from Mainz. When Krug died in 1856, he was buried in Section 8, Block 9, Lot 12 of Forest Home Cemetery, one of Milwaukee's finest final resting places. When Krug's will was submitted in probate, Judge Byron Paine found a total of $15,296.76 in claims and demands against Krug's estate. Included were a $1,000.00 note held by the Second Ward Bank; $276.50 owed to Joseph Schlitz; and $730.39 owed to Joseph Uhrig. There were a total of thirty-four individuals or entities filing claims or demands.[8]

In the meantime, the erstwhile Joseph Schlitz had taken over management of Krug's brewery. Krug's bewitching widow, Anna, wasn't in mourning too long. She and Schlitz married in 1858. Not wasting any time, her new husband changed the name of her late husband's brewery to the Jos. Schlitz Brewing Company and incorporated it that same year with a capitalization of $200,000. Schlitz soon was in the real money, churning out upwards of two thousand barrels of beer a year from a facility on Milwaukee's Chestnut Street, now Juneau Avenue.

After working at the Uhrig Brewery, August Uihlein returned to Milwaukee in 1867 and began work at the Schlitz complex. He joined his brothers—Henry, Edward and Alfred—who had come from Germany in the 1860s to also work at the brewery. Beer sales doubled when Joseph Schlitz flooded the Chicago market with his happy beverage, providing trainloads of beer to a city parched after its horrific 1871 fire. Good for Schlitz but bad for the Windy City's breweries, the conflagration destroyed the plants and warehouses of such venerable brewing names as Doyle & Co., Huck, Jerusalem, Lill & Diversey, Metz, Mueller, Sands and K.G. Schmidt.[9]

The growing success of the Milwaukee company encouraged young August Uihlein to seek a wife; on April 20, 1872, he married Emilie Werdehof, daughter of a wealthy Milwaukee merchant.[10] As a business leader, August Uihlein was called "a man of resourceful ability, of notably sound judgment, of broad vision and keen recognition as to the value of culture…his influence on the development of the city has been immeasurable."[11]

Unfortunately, Joseph Schlitz drowned at sea in 1875, when he was returning to the United States from a visit to Germany. He was aboard the SS *Schiller*, which sank off the coast of England, one of the 335 victims of what is considered one of peacetime's greatest maritime disasters. The brewer was listed as "president of a banking association in Milwaukee" in stories carried by the *New York Times*.[12] At the time of his death, Schlitz was one

In 1850, at age eight, August Uihlein came to the United States with his grandfather, August Krug. Surviving a shipwreck on the way, Uihlein went on to become secretary and chairman of the board of Jos. Schlitz Brewing Company from 1874 to 1911. He was prominent in Milwaukee banking and real estate circles. *Photo courtesy of Lynde Uihlein and the Uihlein family.*

of Milwaukee's richest men, and his company was brewing almost seventy thousand barrels of beer a year.

Luckily for the Uihleins, Schlitz had made out his will before the voyage. The document stipulated that upon his death, the brewery operations would be turned over to August Uihlein, who received 500 shares in the brewery.[13] The again-widowed Anna Krug Schlitz received 2,000 shares, while August's brothers, Henry, Alfred and Edward, each received 250 shares.

Supposedly, the will also stipulated that the business could never remove "Joseph Schlitz" from its title. However, the original will has disappeared from the Milwaukee County Courthouse, and a microfilm version in the archives has been damaged over time so that most of its verbiage is unreadable. As Schlitz historian Leonard Jurgensen once said, the most likely explanation for why the name remained is: "Why is change a good thing?"[14] Subsequently, after Schlitz's burial in the "Beer Barons' Corner" of Milwaukee's Forest Home Cemetery, not far from the crypts of the Blatz and Pabst brewing families, the Uihlein boys were officially in charge at Jos. Schlitz Brewing Company. When Anna Krug Schlitz died in 1887, most of her stock was purchased by the Uihleins.[15]

With Bavarian gusto, the Uihleins capitalized on their heritage to attract customers. They opened Schlitz-only taverns on many Milwaukee street corners and constructed several magnificent beer gardens. One huge hall at Eighth and Walnut Streets featured a wide range of entertainment, from opera performed by the Bach-Luning Orchestra to Turnverien tumbling demonstrations. Tivoli Palm Garden at 729 South Fifth Street was another popular spot. With the entrance decorated with the Jos. Schlitz Brewing Company trademark globe, the building was a companion to the Schlitz Palm Garden downtown at the Schlitz Hotel. The brick and Bedford stone building on the South Side later housed a café, as well as bowling alleys and a barbershop.[16] Today, the structure is home of the Milwaukee Ballet Company, well equipped with offices, four dance studios, a costume shop and plenty of storage space for its more than three thousand costumes.[17]

One of the few entertainment palaces actually bearing the Uihlein name was the Uihlein Theater, a magnificent palace offering three thousand seats on three levels, eighteen luxury boxes flanking the stage and a check room for bicycles on the second floor. It had four bars to serve copious amounts of Schlitz beer when it was opened in 1896 at 334 West Grand Avenue (now Wisconsin Avenue). The Uihleins spent about $500,000 on the construction. However, only a few months later, the name was changed to the Alhambra because the brothers felt their name was too difficult to pronounce. It became a movie theater in 1911 and was demolished in the name of progress in 1959.[18]

After Schlitz's death, August became secretary and chairman of the Schlitz board, holding sway there for the next forty years. He went on to be president of the Second Ward Bank, where he had started his business career three decades earlier. He was also considered one of Milwaukee's prime real estate moguls, in addition to owning real estate in Chicago and New York City.[19] The Uihleins also managed hotels in Winona, Minnesota, and Omaha, Nebraska.[20]

August's brother, Henry, learned the brewing business in Germany. He immigrated to the United States in 1862, working for several years in various breweries in St. Louis and in Leavenworth, Kansas. In 1871, he also moved to Milwaukee to join his brothers at Jos. Schlitz. Henry was president of the brewery from 1875 to 1916 and was involved with the family's growing banking, real estate and financial ventures.

Alfred Eugene Uihlein, the third brother, was also born in Baden, Germany, migrating to America in 1867. As did Henry, Alfred worked in St. Louis; Carrollton, Illinois; and Leavenworth, coming to Milwaukee in 1871. He was superintendent at Jos. Schlitz from 1874 to 1916 and succeeded his brother Henry as president of the firm in 1916. He served as president until his retirement in 1926. August Uihlein was secretary and chairman of the board at Schlitz from 1874 to his death in 1911 and was also prominent in Wisconsin banking and real estate. By coincidence, August became chair at Schlitz the same year as the founding of the Women's Christian Temperance Union (WCTU) in Cleveland.[21] August was also Milwaukee's richest man, owning the largest chunk of stock in the company.[22]

The Uihleins were constantly on the lookout for improving their product and were quick to seize on new ways of operating and brewing. In 1883,

Danish biochemist Emil Christian Hansen, a scientist for the Carlsberg laboratories in Copenhagen, demonstrated how various yeasts were harmful to proper fermentation. He subsequently produced a special yeast culture specifically for beer making, a process then used at Carlsberg. That same year, William J. Uihlein, son of Alfred, brought Hansen's special culture to Milwaukee and started using it. Schlitz thus got the jump on the Pabst Brewery, which didn't use the special ingredient until 1887, when it also acquired the formula.[23]

William Uihlein, who was trained as a mechanical engineer, worked his way up at the brewery, eventually succeeding Alfred as chairman of the Jos. Schlitz board in 1933 before retiring three years later.

He and his wife, Melitta, purchased a mansion in Naples, Florida, in 1937 as part of an influx of wealthy Milwaukeeans who vacationed in the area.[24]

As mentioned earlier, the growing success of the brewery had encouraged young August Uihlein to seek a wife, and he married Emilie Werdehof on April 20, 1872. Among their children, Joseph (Joe) Edgar Uihlein Sr. was born on December 23, 1875, in the family home at North Fourth and Walnut Streets. To his eventual brood of grandchildren, Joseph Sr. was more commonly known as "Opa," the affectionate German word for "grandfather."[25] Joseph E. Uihlein Sr. had begun working at the brewery when he was seventeen, starting as an apprentice in 1882, so he was not a stranger to the trade. After studying brewing at the Alfred Jorgensen fermentation laboratory in Copenhagen, he attended Sanford University. Joseph left there to finish college at Cornell University, graduating with a bachelor of laws degree in 1901 and returning to Schlitz.

Throughout their professional careers, the Uihleins were always promotions conscious, looking for every opportunity

Joseph E. Uihlein Sr. (1875–1968) was named general manager of the Jos. Schlitz Brewing Company in 1906 and vice-president in 1912. He retired in 1945. Uihlein was also chairman of the Second Ward Savings Bank when it merged with First Wisconsin National Bank in 1928 and a director of First Wisconsin until 1949. *Photo courtesy of Lynde Uihlein and the Uihlein family.*

Joseph E. Uihlein's 3318 Lake Drive property was designed by the dynamic architectural duo of Charles Kirschoff and Thomas Rose, Milwaukee's most important building design firm between 1897 and 1973. Over the generations, Kirschoff and Rose developed about three thousand structures throughout the community, including at least two hundred taverns for the Jos. Schlitz Brewing Co. *Photo courtesy of Lynde Uihlein and the Uihlein family.*

to pitch their brew. Under their direction, the brewery sent a shipload of Schlitz beer to soldiers and sailors in the Philippines after Admiral George Dewey defeated the Spanish fleet in Manila Bay on May 1, 1898.[26] As early as 1900, the brewery had also begun distributing its beer via refrigerated rail cars, brightly painted for the company's logo. Schlitz favored the bright yellow Union Refrigerator (URTX) cars. However, when there was a rail car shortage, its beer occasionally had to be transported in a carrier painted with another company's message. In the late 1930s, however, the Federal Trade Commission prohibited any advertising on the sides of refrigerator cars.[27] These initial marketing efforts paid off. By late 1902, the brewery was among the world's largest beer producers, with an annual output of more than one million barrels.[28]

After graduation, Joseph met the lovely Ilma Louis Vogel, a much-sought-after Milwaukee socialite who was born on September 26, 1885.

Her grandfather, Frederick Vogel Sr., had moved to Milwaukee from Buffalo, New York, in 1847. Lured to Milwaukee because of its business opportunities and large German population, the elder Vogel had started a tanning plant in partnership with fellow émigré entrepreneur Guido Pfister.

In fine style, Joe and Ilma married in 1904. Confident in his son's business abilities, August Uihlein made Joseph the general manager of

The gate entrance of the Joseph Uihlein home on Milwaukee's Lake Drive is still a city landmark. *Photo courtesy of Lynde Uihlein and the Uihlein family.*

Opposite, top: Children ice-skated in front of the Joseph Uihlein home on Milwaukee's upscale Lake Drive. The unit at the far right was the "playhouse," topped by a whimsical bear statue on the chimney. The building is now a condo. *Photo courtesy of Lynde Uihlein and the Uihlein family.*

Opposite, bottom: The paneled dining room of the Joseph Uihlein residence in Milwaukee was typical of the interior design favored by the city's brewers, many of whom emigrated from Germany. *Photo courtesy of Lynde Uihlein and the Uihlein family.*

Schlitz in 1906 at age thirty-one. Two years later, the company built another brewery in Cleveland, which added more oversight responsibilities for the younger Uihlein.[29]

In addition to his brewing duties, Joseph Uihlein had many auxiliary business interests. Among them, he was president of the Second Ward Bank from 1911 until 1928, when it merged with the First Wisconsin at the onset of the Great Depression. Other banks involved in this lifesaving merger included the Pabst-owned Wisconsin National Bank and the Germania National Bank, under the control of Uihlein's sister, Thekla.

This formidable female presence was also known as "Big T," "Big Tek" or "Steamboat." Typical of the era when Milwaukee's upper crust merged with one another's families, Thekla was married to Milwaukee financier William Brumder, son of George Brumder, who headed one of the nation's largest German-language publishing businesses.[30]

August Uihlein died on October 11, 1911, while vacationing on the island of Helgoland in the southeastern corner of the North Sea. Upon August's death, Joseph inherited a one-seventeenth share of the stock of the brewery, as did each of his siblings. Joseph's brother, Robert, was also a skilled brewer who honed his craft at the Wahl-Henius brewer's institute in Chicago and the Alfred Joergersen Laboratories. With this background, his knowledge of bacteriology and yeast culture was important when he joined the brewery in 1908. He became secretary of the firm in 1910, a director in 1912 and vice-president in 1918. He remained in those positions until his death in 1959.[31]

Joseph Uihlein was a fair but hard taskmaster, pushing Schlitz to achieve even greater production and distribution. Always the amateur engineer and supporter of all things scientific, he encouraged numerous advances in the industry, including enzymatic control in the brewing process, elimination of air from bottles prior to filling, addition of vitamins to the beer and several technical improvements in bottling and packaging. Under his direction, the brewery introduced its famous brown bottle about 1911, a pioneering move that prevented harmful light rays from affecting the quality and stability of its contents.

Under his leadership, Schlitz survived even Prohibition and the Great Depression by capitalizing on wise land investments, expanding its banking interests, starting up an aluminum venture, selling its interest in the American Tobacco Co. and manufacturing malt syrup for cooking, baking and the production of soft drinks.[32]

Generally, Joseph Uihlein got along well with his workers, always saying that what was good for them was good for business. Yet his goodwill was stretched thin in the spring of 1922, when negotiations collapsed between Milwaukee's brewers and their workers. The companies were in a growing financial bind, as the new nonalcoholic products resulted in sluggish sales and profits plummeted as a result of Prohibition. In April, a strike was called against all the Milwaukee breweries, except Blatz, which had signed the union contract demanding a closed shop.

Miller Brewing settled in the autumn of 1923, and non-union laborers replaced the striking workers at Schlitz and Pabst, resulting in a boycott of their products. In the middle of 1925, however, the Schlitz stockholders agreed to sign a contract, hoping to gain advantage over their competitors. This action broke the united front of the breweries, and they capitulated to the workers' demands by 1926. An eight-hour day, compulsory arbitration and a new wage system were devised. Qualified workers could make twenty-nine to thirty-one dollars for a forty-hour week, although women's wages never topped twenty dollars a week.[33]

Although he was a business conservative, his brothers accused him of being one of those "terrible liberals." Yet Joseph Uihlein did what he needed to do to advance the financial interests of both the family and brewery. He was a realist and approachable when it came to work issues and had no problem dealing with the unions and Social Democrats who ran Milwaukee's government during his brewery management years. Always interested in community affairs, Uihlein was named Milwaukee commissioner of public debt in 1910, appointed by Emil Seidel, a patternmaker who became the city's first Social Democrat (Socialist) mayor. Seidel won election in a landslide. His campaign was based on a "workingman's platform" but was also eager to reach out to business leaders like Uihlein. In his position, Uihlein followed in the footsteps of the city's other notable commissioners of public debt. They included the peripatetic Alexander Mitchell (1861 to 1865) and Guido Pfister (1871 to 1886), who constructed the Pfister Hotel and was business partner with Frederick Vogel Sr., his wife's grandfather.

Always a confirmed Republican, Uihlein was one of the few non Social Democrats in a city hall/county courthouse crowd that numbered twenty-one Socialists out of thirty-five aldermen, ten out of sixteen county supervisors and two judges. In his governmental appointment, Uihlein probably needed to deal with Seidel's secretary, Carl Sandburg, who ultimately went on to be one of America's greatest poets. As a young man, Sandburg was well known in the city's political circles and was a hardworking Social Democrat organizer.[34]

Following Prohibition, in the spring of 1933, Joseph turned over the company leadership to his brother Erwin. The brewery immediately began modernizing and expanding its facilities. By 1934, the brewery had ramped up production and turned out one million barrels of beer.[35] Following the lead of other breweries, the firm began using flattop cans produced by the Continental Can Company in addition to its kegs.[36] The company started with a twelve-ounce can, followed in 1954 with a sixteen-fluid-ounce container. In 1963, it introduced the industry's first "easy-opening" tab top.[37]

In the early and mid-1950s, Schlitz continued to grow, even as dark clouds loomed on its financial horizon and beer markets began changing in post–World War II America. Forging ahead, in 1954, Schlitz constructed a new brewery on Woodman Avenue in Van Nuys, a small city in the San Fernando Valley. In 1956, it then acquired the old Muehlback Brewery in Kansas City. A year later, the firm built a $20 million brewery in Tampa.[38]

When the Uihlein descendants gathered for a reunion, it made quite a crowd. Their ancestors formed the early management team at the Jos. Schlitz Brewing Company. *Photo courtesy of Lynde Uihlein and the Uihlein family.*

Spending about $106 million to build facilities, including four of the largest grain elevators in the world, and to purchase modernized equipment, Erwin ultimately bolstered the company's assets. Ever frugal during his tenure, he achieved this feat without using credit or going into debt. Because of Erwin's success, building on what his brother Joseph had done, the Schlitz brewery climbed back to its position as the United States' second-largest producer of beer in the 1950s and 1960s yet still lagged behind Anheuser-Busch.[39]

When Erwin's nephew, Robert Uihlein Jr., took over as president in 1961, Erwin stayed active in management affairs and headed the Schlitz Brewing Company, Limited, in Toronto. Erwin was also a big player in Milwaukee banking and real estate circles. Robert Jr., a polo and tennis aficionado, as well as a big game hunter, had been named a Schlitz vice-president in 1945. When he replaced Erwin, young Bob's competitive streak attempted to jolt Schlitz out of its second place status. It was a difficult pitch, since Erwin stayed on as chairman of the board until 1967, at a time when Schlitz was churning out eleven million barrels of beer a year. Satisfied with this volume, the older man was set in his ways of running the brewery.[40]

With a growing demand for beer, the firm wanted to produce more product and subsequently tightened up the fermenting process. This resulted in quality-control issues, with Schlitz beer going flat quickly, losing its punch and flavor. Drinkers weren't pleased when a seaweed extract called propylene glycol alginate was added to the mash in an effort to fix the flatness problem and return fizz to the beer. But after bottles and kegs were warehoused for a few months, the concoction turned into a solid, chunky crud nicknamed "Schlitz Bits." This condition naturally drove away fastidious beer drinkers, even if they were longtime Schlitz fans.[11]

The firm also tried to save money in the brewing process by using cheaper corn syrup instead of the more expensive barley malt. That was another contributing factor to the decline in customers, who were also turned off by an aggressive marketing campaign daring anyone to "take away my gusto." The firm was as slow in recognizing the rise in demand for light beer.[12] Seeking diversification, Schlitz wanted to increase the market for its spent grain. L.A. Hunt, assistant to the vice-president of brewing and manager of the grain department at the brewery, developed the idea of "Brewers Wet Grains." In 1966, Murphy Products Company and Schlitz began developing Maltlage, a branded version of brewers' grain silage.[13]

In the early 1970s, Schlitz and Anheuser-Busch remained North America's leaders in the beer business, owning fourteen breweries between them, each producing ten to twelve million barrels of beverage a year. However, Anheuser-Busch remained the alpha dog, whose plants continued to turn out about a million more barrels a year than the Milwaukee-headquartered company.[14] As drinkers departed the label, Schlitz's market share plunged from 18 percent in 1970 to barely 4 percent in 1978. Robert Jr. "bet the farm" on a new ad push claiming that Schlitz offered "real gusto in a light beer," following Miller's lead for branding product. He went on a diversifying binge that included $100 million dropped into a Chilean fishing fleet and purchased breweries in Turkey, Belgium, Puerto Rico and Spain.[15] He also arranged for Schlitz to sponsor the Great Circus Parade in Milwaukee, using historical wagons from the Circus World Museum in Baraboo, Wisconsin.[16] In 1954, Schlitz was number 291 on the first-ever Fortune 500 list, following Pabst at the 216 mark. But by 1980, Schlitz had slipped to 328, still edging out rival Pabst at 378.[17]

There were management shakeups at the brewery following the death, in 1976, of Robert Jr., who had been chairman of the Schlitz board since 1967. He was replaced by Daniel F. (Jack) McKeithan Jr., who held the position until 1982. In 1979, Schlitz brewed about 10 percent of the nation's beer but continued to lose money. Despite the effects of a bitter strike in the Milwaukee brewery in 1981, which resulted in the closing of the brewery, Schlitz continued producing all its products in other plants throughout the United States. However, in March 1982, Stroh Brewing Company of Detroit initiated a two-tier tender offer directly to the stockholders, offering cash for the majority of the shares, a move made against the recommendation of the company's management and board. McKeithan and other corporate officers contacted major stockholders around the country, urging them not to accept the Stroh bid. Yet after an epic court battle that was resolved in surprisingly quick fashion, Stroh's tactic was successful. In effect, the Detroiters bought the Milwaukee company directly from the stockholders for $500 million when they raised their offer from an initial $16 per share to $17. With Schlitz safely tucked in its corporate back pocket, Stroh became the United States' third-largest brewery. The Milwaukee headquarters were subsequently shuttered, stunning the general Milwaukee community. Stroh then also unloaded many of Schlitz's plants to pay for the acquisition and concentrated on promoting its secondary brand, Old Milwaukee.[18]

Schlitz returned to the scene in 2008, courtesy of Pabst Brewing Co., which had owned the Schlitz brand since 1999 and now contracts with MillerCoors LLC for its brewing. In 2007, Pabst test marketed the old formula for Schlitz, calling it Classic 1960s, and made it available in bottles.[19] Early in 2010, Schlitz beer was again being sold in its signature "Tall Boy" cans and earned its place on the shelves once more.[50]

Pabst Brewing Company

Experiencing the political turmoil of Europe in 1849, Gottleib Pabst decided to seek his fortune in America. Along with his wife, Frederika, and twelve-year-old son, Frederick, he departed their hometown of Nikolausrieth, Thuringia. The trio headed to the port of Hamburg, where the elder Pabst sailed off first to make arrangements in the United States, booking a second passage for the rest of the family to come later. Reunited in New York, the family made their way to Milwaukee, a journey of at least thirty-three days up the Hudson to the St. Lawrence River and across the Great Lakes. One leg of the trip was probably aboard a passenger vessel owned by the Ward Line, one of the largest carriers of the era.[51]

Above, left: Frederick Pabst in 1856, his earliest known photo. *Photo courtesy of the Historic Pabst Mansion.*

Above, right: Captain Frederick Pabst. *Photo courtesy of the Historic Pabst Mansion.*

When the Pabsts arrived in rough-and-tumble frontier Milwaukee in the autumn of 1848, Gottleib Pabst wasn't keen on what he saw, despite the growing number of other German immigrants there. Instead of settling in, he decided to move to Chicago, where, unfortunately, Fredericka died in a cholera epidemic the next year. Gottleib worked as a waiter at the Mansion House Hotel, while young Frederick landed a job as a busboy for five dollars a month and room and board. But the lure of adventure was too much. Frederick soon shipped out on one of the Ward Line ships as a cabin boy, probably smitten by the thrill of sailing on his journey to Milwaukee. Pabst eventually became a first mate and was hired by the Goodrich Transportation Line in 1858, becoming a captain at the age of twenty-three. He proudly retained that title for the remainder of his life.[52]

The vessels he commanded carried everything from leather hides to molasses and barrels of whiskey, along with passengers.[53] One of his ships, the *Comet*, was elegantly furnished and considered among the fanciest passenger vessels on Lake Michigan. Among the regular voyageurs was Phillip Best, who owned a small brewery in Milwaukee. On occasional business trips, he brought along his daughter, Maria. The young couple hit it off and began a courtship, encouraged by Best, who probably saw a future business partner as well as a son-in-law. Thus did parental units think in those days.

In 1842, Best's two brothers, Jacob Jr. and Charles, had immigrated to Milwaukee from their home in Mettenheim, Germany. They immediately opened a vinegar distillery but switched to more lucrative beer brewing in 1844. The hardworking brothers produced about three hundred barrels of beer in their first year, calling their firm the Empire Brewing Company. Also in 1844, their father, Jacob Sr., and their brothers Lorenz and the aforementioned Phillip, who was accompanied by his wife and baby daughter, Maria, joined them. Once ensconced in Wisconsin, they joined Jacob Jr. and Charles in the brewery, now called Jacob Best and Sons.

Yet business disputes between the brothers led Charles and Lorenz to leave in 1850 to start the Plank Road Brewery. The business was not successful, so it was sold to Frederick Miller, who renamed it after himself.

Jacob Best Sr. retired in 1853, leaving Jacob Jr. and Phillip to run the operation. Phillip bought out his remaining brother in 1859, deciding to manage the brewing alone. Yet it was a strenuous, complex job, so it was no wonder that when a dashing lake captain showed an interest in his daughter, Phillip Best encouraged the romance. Despite the onslaught of the Civil War, Pabst and Maria married on March 25, 1862. Pabst continued sailing for a couple of years, but his father-in-law eventually convinced him to try his hand at the brewery. As added incentive, in 1864, Phillip Best sold half his operations to Pabst, who became company vice-president.

Two years later, Phillip's younger daughter, Lisette, married Emil Schandein, a traveling salesman who had come to America from Bavaria in 1856. Shortly after the couple was married, Phillip Best sold his half of the brewery to Schandein, with Pabst remaining as president and the new son-in-law assuming the position of vice-president. Phillip Best moved back to Germany, where he died in 1869.

The two owners of the Best Brewery made a great team. In their first expansion move, they purchased the former Melms Brewing Company, with Schandein placed in charge there. In March 1873, the Phillip Best Brewing Company was producing 100,593 barrels a year, already making it one of the top breweries in the country. Captain and Mrs. Pabst were also busy on the homefront, with five children in the family: Elizabeth, Gustave, Marie, Frederick Jr. and Emma. He purchased a large farm in the suburb of Wauwatosa, where he raised Percheron horses for teams hauling his beer wagons. The farm was also handy for turning loose the Pabst kids in the summer.[54]

In 1882, the market-savvy partners began tying blue silk ribbons around the necks of their Select-brand beer. While it never actually won a blue ribbon prize in any competition, the gimmick caught on and was used until 1916. The brand was eventually officially renamed Pabst Blue Ribbon in 1896.[55] Pabst and Schandein were also interested in the latest technology, both in the brewing process and generally in anything that would help their business. They added a Western Union telegraph office to their headquarters, built mechanical refrigeration facilities and installed incandescent lightbulbs. The firm suffered a setback in 1888, when Schandein died suddenly while on a business trip to Germany. With this vacuum in management, Schandein's wife, Lisette, Pabst's sister-in-law, became the brewery's vice-president. This made her one of the few female executives of her era, although she did not have a hand in the day-to-day running of the company. Charles Best, Phillip Best's nephew, was secretary at the time.[56]

On March 12, 1889, the brewery's board voted to rename the firm the Pabst Brewing Company, a move that did not require any change in the company's direction, since Captain Pabst was already president. The firm's hop-leaf corporate logo remained the same. In an interesting word twist, the company motto became "He drinks best who drinks Pabst," for a wink and a nod to both the Best and the Pabst families. With both business and family proceeding along smartly, Pabst decided to build a home befitting his growing stature. In 1889, he commissioned Milwaukee architects George Bowman Ferry and Alfred Charles Clas to design a substantial mansion in the Flemish Renaissance Revival style. The imposing structure, one of the finest in the city, was completed in 1892. It was close enough to his work that he could get up early, visit the brewery and be home for lunch. After lunch, Pabst would head back to the office, usually working until about 6:00 p.m.[57] By 1890, the brewery complex covered six full city blocks, making it one of Milwaukee's largest industries with its own fire, advertising and architecture departments.

Captain Pabst was a true community leader, active in philanthropic and social affairs. One of his major projects was the Das Neue Deutsche Stadt-Theater (the New German City Theater), which he purchased and renovated in 1890. When the building was damaged in a fire in 1895, it was rebuilt and renamed as the Pabst Theater, designed by architect Otto Strack much like one of the great European opera houses. Still a Milwaukee landmark, the Baroque interior includes an Austrian crystal chandelier, a staircase made of white Italian Carrara marble and a proscenium arch highlighted in gold leaf framing the stage.[58] He also built the tallest building in Milwaukee of the day,

The Pabsts are ready for an outing in the summer of 1896, with a carriage parked outside their palatial home. *Photo courtesy of the Historic Pabst Mansion.*

the ornate sixteen-story Pabst Building on the east bank of the Milwaukee River, and the St. Charles Hotel, along with hotels and offices in New York, Minneapolis, Chicago and other cities.

Pabst initiated brewery tours, hosting thousands of visitors a year. One guest, a visiting congressman, thought he'd pull a joke when he ordered a Schlitz beer after a walk around the brewery. Yet Pabst immediately had the requested iced beverage from his competitor delivered to the politician's table. With a laugh, Pabst indicated that he always kept plenty of other brands on hand in the tour center for just such occasions.[59] Pabst, by the way, was more of a wine connoisseur than a beer man when it came to meals or social occasions.[60]

To accommodate the ballooning demand for Pabst, dozens of train cars packed with product rolled out of the company's own shipping depot on a daily basis and utilized its own dock on the Milwaukee River. To be sure of a steady supply of energy for its operations, the brewery constructed the Pabst Heat, Light & Power Company on Broadway Street. In 1893, Pabst

The Pabst Pavilion at the Columbian Exposition was moved by Captain Pabst to the grounds of his Milwaukee home after the fair in 1894. The structure is now the Historic Pabst Mansion gift shop. *Photo courtesy of the Historic Pabst Mansion.*

Wagons loaded with beer are ready to roll out from the Pabst Brewery dispatch yard in 1900. *Photo courtesy of the Historic Pabst Mansion.*

was awarded the beer concession for the World's Columbian Exposition in Chicago and earned a "best" beer honor. It was one more step to ensure that by 1900, Pabst had become a major household name. Two years later, Pabst became the largest brewery in the country, selling between 900,000 and 1 million barrels a year.[61]

Pabst survived two strokes in 1903 and decided to relinquish control of the brewery to his children, signing the necessary papers, a will and the stock certificates to complete the transaction. He said he took the action "principally as a test and incidentally to rid himself of business cares" and to see "how the responsibility of wealth would rest on [his children's] shoulders."[62] Captain Pabst died on January 1, 1904, with his son Gustave taking the reins as president on January 11; Gustave remained in that office until December 23, 1921, when Frederick's younger son, Fred Jr., became president.

As with other brewery titans, Pabst needed to change focus when Prohibition hit. It made cheese, acquired the Sheboygan Beverage Company to produce soft drinks and snapped up the Chicago-based Puritan Malt Extract Company in 1930.[63] After Prohibition's repeal, Pabst merged with the Premier Malt Products Company of Peoria, Illinois, with Premier's chief executive, Harris Perlstein, named to head the Milwaukee brewery. The new firm was called Premier-Pabst Corporation. Perlstein guided his new company back to first place in the country's brewing world. In 1934, it picked up a brewing facility in Peoria Heights, Illinois, and then opened a third plant in Newark, New Jersey, and began selling beer in cans, the only major brewer to do so. The board then decided to return to the original Pabst brewing corporate title in 1938. In 1948, it purchased the Los Angeles

The Pabst logo has long been a symbol of great Milwaukee beer. *Photo courtesy of the Historic Pabst Mansion.*

Brewing Company and set its eyes on other possibilities. Fred Pabst was chairman of the board until retiring in 1954.

By 1958, the Pabst family was hoping to return to control of the brewery that bore their name. The Pabst stockholders tried to dump Perlstein, who in turn kept expanding. He plunked Milwaukee's Blatz Brewery into the corporate basket, with its president, James Windham, becoming Pabst president. In 1972, Windham made his own way to the corner office, as chairman and chief executive officer, while former Marquette University law professor Frank DeGuire became Pabst president, serving for ten years.[64]

Windham pulled Pabst back into a third place ranking in beer production a few years after taking control of the brewery. Production and sales went from 1.9 million barrels in 1960 to 12.6 million in 1972. By this time, Pabst had gotten rid of Blatz, selling that branch off to G. Heileman Brewing in La Crosse, Wisconsin, in 1969. After buying up some brands produced by the Hamm Brewing company in 1975, sales of Pabst peaked in 1977, when they reached 18 million barrels.[65] Yet by the early 1980s, sales slumped again, and numerous executives got the axe. Five plants were shuttered and sold off to G. Heileman.

In 1985, Paul Kalmanovitz, a so-called "self-made beer and real-estate baron," as well as a notorious cost cutter, purchased the original Pabst company for $63 million. Kalmanovitz created S&P—the "P" referred to his nickname, "Mr. Paul," and the "S" referred to one-time partner Nathan Sherry—as the holding company. S&P's first acquisition was Maier Brewing Company, purchased in 1958. Kalmanovitz died in 1987, and the Kalmanovitz Charitable Foundation then controlled Pabst Brewing. Kalmanovitz's successor, Lutz Issleib, slashed the advertising budget and deferred capital investment, hoping that Captain Pabst's past glory would generate profits.

The strategy obviously failed, so the brewery continued to slide downhill, causing it to close its Milwaukee plant in 1996. At the time, Pabst still had the fourth-largest U.S. beer operation in 1998, producing 13.5 million barrels. But by the end of 2007, Pabst, which had more than $600 million in annual sales and produced thirty-six different beers, was sixth, with 6.1 million barrels. By 2001, the brand's sales were below 1 million barrels, 90 percent less than the peak.[66] S&P Company was ordered by the IRS to sell the Pabst by 2005 or lose its not-for-profit, tax-free status. The company claimed that it was unable to find a buyer at market value and requested an extension until 2010, which the IRS granted.[67]

Food magnate C. Dean Metropoulos finally stepped in and purchased Pabst for about $250 million on May 26, 2010.[68]

In 2011, Pabst was headquartered in Woodridge, Illinois, a Chicago suburb. The current holding company portfolio showed that it contracts for the brewing of more than two dozen brands of beer and malt liquor from long-gone companies, including G. Heileman Brewing Company, Lone Star Brewing Company, Pearl Brewing Company, Piels Bros., National Brewing Company, Primo Brewing & Malting Company, Rainier Brewing Company, F&M Schaefer Brewing Company, Joseph Schlitz Brewing Company and Stroh Brewery Company. The company also brews Ice Man Malt Liquor, St. Ides High Gravity Malt Liquor and retail versions of beers from McSorley's Old Ale House and Southampton Publick House. Pabst itself is contract brewed in six different breweries around the United States in facilities owned by Miller Brewing Company.[69]

Captain Pabst's magnificent home is now a major Milwaukee tourism destination, located at 2000 West Wisconsin Avenue. In May 1908, the archdiocese of Milwaukee purchased the residence for use by the archbishop.

Philanthropist and developer Joe Zilber (center, to right of man in vest) stands with his renovation crew outside the historic Pabst brewery in Milwaukee. In August 2006, Zilber's investment group, Brewery Project LLC, purchased the old buildings for $13 million to create a residential, office and retail complex. *Photo courtesy of Zilber Ltd.*

In 1975, the mansion was to be sold and scheduled for demolition, until local entrepreneur John Conlan rescued it. The building was purchased and renovated by Wisconsin Heritages, Inc., opening for tours in 1978. In the summer of 1998, the board of directors officially renamed the organization Captain Frederick Pabst Mansion, Inc., to reflect the renewed focus solely on the restoration of the Pabst Mansion and the preservation of the Pabst Family legacy.[70]

By 2011, the remains of Pabst brewery have undergone numerous transitions, including the establishment of the Best Place Tavern in the old visitors' center at 901 West Juneau Avenue, renovation for office space and even being rented out for period films. The process of neighborhood revitalization was pushed by the late Joseph Zilber, a community developer and philanthropist who had purchased the sprawling complex in 2005.[71]

MILLER BREWING COMPANY, NOW MILLERCOORS

The founder of the Miller Brewing Company, Frederick Miller, was born into a middle-class family in 1824 in Riedlingen, a village in southwest Germany in a region noted for its breweries.[72] So it seemed natural that he secured a job in the industry as a young man, working for a succession of small master brewers to gain experience. In 1849, he leased the Royal Brewery at Sigmaringen, home of the Hohenzollern princes. Miller brewed beer under a royal license that indicated "by gracious permission of his highness." With a successful business, he made a marriageable catch in Josephine Miller, a local mason's daughter. With the same last name, the match was perfect. Their first son, Joseph Edward, was born in 1854, the same year that the young couple decided to sell their lease and seek a new life in the United States. With his background, Miller sought to establish another brewery and probably considered Milwaukee as a promising locale because of the high percentage of Germans living there.[73]

In 1855, Miller purchased a mortgage for the Plank Road Brewery and completed the acquisition the next year. The brewery had been founded by Charles and Lorenz Best, brothers whose family also owned the Jacob Best Brewing Company, forerunner of Pabst Brewing. Miller capitalized on the Bests' "cave system" of storage for beer, keeping the full barrels in a cool, quiet locale so the beer could settle for several months after brewing. Miller improved on the technique, lining the caves with brick and expanding their

Above, left: Jacob Leinenkugel, who owned half the breweries in Chippewa Falls, Wisconsin, first met Frederick Miller when the Milwaukee brewer visited the North Woods in 1885. About a century later, Miller purchased Leinenkugel's brewery. *Photo courtesy of Miller/Coors-Milwaukee.*

Above, right: Frederick Miller. *Photo courtesy of Miller/Coors-Milwaukee.*

capacity to twelve thousand barrels. The system was so successful that the brewery used the caves until 1906, when refrigerator facilities took over.[71]

Miller ran a tight ship, keeping a close eye on expenditures in meticulously inscribed ledgers. It is said that he got out of bed at 4:00 a.m. and often worked nonstop until 9:00 p.m. as he built up his customer base. His first customers included the Wauwatosa House hotel, where he sold a quarter barrel of beer for $1.75; a local stone quarry; the Milwaukee County poor farm; and other nearby businesses.[75] Other neighbors just down the Plank Road were the Schweickhart Brewery, the forerunner of the Gettelman Brewery, and the Spring Street Distillery, which made wine and whiskey. Eventually, however, the ever-growing Miller operation absorbed both properties. It wasn't long before Miller was looking for markets beyond Milwaukee, eyeing Chicago, St. Louis and more distant opportunities wherever Germans had settled.

Miller's wife, Josephine, died in 1860. The couple had six children, most of whom did not survive infancy. One daughter, Louisa, died of tuberculosis at the age of sixteen. He married Lisette Gross six months later, and together they had five children who lived to adulthood. Miller himself died of cancer on June 11, 1888, and his surviving sons, Ernest, Emil and Frederick A., along with their brother-in-law, Carl, took over the company, which was incorporated as the Frederick Miller Brewing Company. Marketing as early as 1903 included Miller High Life, called the "Champagne of Bottled Beer," and the fabled Girl in the Moon four years later. By 1916, production had soared to 450,000 barrels, a drive that crashed into the roadblock of Prohibition. The company managed to survive by producing cereal beverages, soft drinks and malt-related products.[76]

Ernest Miller died in 1925 and was succeeded as president by his brother, Frederick A. Miller. Frederick A. was later succeeded by his sister, Elise K. John, and then by his nephew Harry G. John Jr. In 1947, his nephew Frederick C. became head of the firm. Frederick C. launched a hearty expansion program, but his death and that of his twenty-one-year-old son, Fred Jr., in a plane crash in Milwaukee in 1954 was a blow to the company. At the time, Miller was ranked ninth among American breweries. Norman Klug, the brewery's general counsel, who became president following Miller's death, and the first non-Miller family member to head the company, donned Frederick C.'s mantle and launched a buying spree. Under Klug, the A. Gettelman Company was purchased in 1961, and others followed.[77]

Before Klug's death in 1966, arrangements had been made for a diversified shipping firm, W.R. Grace, to acquire 53 percent of the brewing company. J. Peter Grace, then that company's president, was a longtime family friend of the Millers. He was also treasurer of the De Rancé Foundation, which had been established by Harry John Jr., and one of the two members representing the charity on the brewery's board. Mrs. Lorraine Mulberger and her family and De Rancé owned the Miller stock at that time because Lorraine's brother, Harry John, had donated his 47 percent share of Miller stock to this foundation. The Mulbergers were paid $36 million. Because of its cash reserves and expanding importance within the industry, Miller was a prime

Norman Klug, president of Miller. *Photo courtesy of Miller/Coors-Milwaukee.*

acquisition target. In 1969, management at Grace sold its interest in Miller to PepsiCo for $120 million. Grace canceled the agreement and soon after sold its shares to Philip Morris for $130 million. PepsiCo filed suit in federal court to prevent this, but the suit fell through.[78]

Philip Morris bought out the remaining shares of Miller's stock from the De Rancé Foundation in 1970.

By 1972, Miller Brewing ranked seventh in the beer industry. Targeting Anheuser-Busch as the nation's largest brewer, the company expanded the number of brands, and production rose from 7 million barrels in 1973 to 31 million barrels in 1978.

Led by John Murphy, a Philip Morris executive trained as a lawyer and, with notable marketing ability, the company began a thorough study of American beer drinking trends. Miller had been known previously as the "Champagne of Beers," and its advertising campaigns were directed to appeal to a specific group of white-collar consumers. Murphy revised the old "champagne" marketing strategy and aimed it at what it saw as a vastly larger blue-collar market. Miller's new slogan was: "If you've got the time, we've got the beer." This slogan, combined with aggressive marketing, actually led to increased sales.[79]

By 1985, reduced calorie beers accounted for 20.5 percent of all beer sales. Miller initiated this market with Miller Lite, which is still a major-selling beer in this category, stressing its lower calorie content and its special flavor. Shortly after the introduction of Miller Lite, the company successfully marketed a domestically brewed version of Löwenbräu, a highly regarded German beer for which Miller owned the American distribution rights. As a result, these various brands, including the new Miller Genuine Draft and budget beers Meister Brau and Milwaukee's Best, placed Miller in second place behind Anheuser-Busch by the early 1980s. Early in 1988, Miller's president and chief executive William Howell took an early retirement, being replaced by Leonard J. Goldstein, a senior vice-president with much marketing experience.

Goldstein hit the beer road running. In 1988, he purchased the venerable Jacob Leinenkeugel Brewing Company from Chippewa Falls, Wisconsin. The small 120-year-old facility gave Miller a toehold in the by-now exploding boutique beer market. The following year, Goldstein was named chairman of the Miller board, succeeded as president by Warren Dunn, who also became chairman of the Beer Institute in 1992. The organization was the industry's major lobbying voice, founded in 1986.[80]

Under Goldstein and Dunn, Miller's market share continued to increase. By 1991, it had risen 23 percent to 43.5 million barrels. But in general, sales

Clockwise from top, left: A bottle of Miller Genuine Draft stands tall and proud, ready for drinking; A tub of iced Miller Genuine Draft is great for a hot day; A Miller Genuine Draft beer sign lights up the night; A cooler packed with Miller Genuine Draft bottles is a welcome sight. *Photos courtesy of Miller/Coors.*

were going flat industry wide. By December 1993, Miller had eliminated 13 percent of its workforce, among whom were three hundred white-collar workers in its Milwaukee headquarters.

That year, in an attempt to compete with Anheuser-Busch in the international market, Miller paid $273 million for U.S. distribution rights and a 20 percent holding in Canada's Molson Breweries. The company further protected itself by purchasing the domestic distribution rights to Fosters Lager and other imported beers and introducing Icehouse and Lite Ice brands.[81]

For six years, company president and former Anheuser-Busch executive Jack McDonough worked hard to pull Miller up higher in the brewing ranks, but he and Miller's marketing and sales vice-presidents John Rooney and Chris Moore were edged out in 1999 because they couldn't quite do the job. McDonough was replaced by John Bowlin, who had been with Philip Morris's Kraft Foods International Division. Bowlin was one of several Kraft Foods International and Philip Morris U.S.A. top managers brought in by Miller parent Philip Morris to halt the brewer's ongoing slide in share and sales. The changes came after a year in which the brewery's profits crept upwards by 1.3 percent to $451 million, despite the fact that sales fell 2.3 percent to $4.1 billion and its share of the United States' beer market dropped 0.7 percentage points to 21.0 percent. Brewery analysts also pointed out that Miller's advertising efforts were not effective and failed to spark new sales. In addition, despite the resurrection of old advertising ideas, sales of Miller Genuine Draft and Miller Lite continued to slip. So the management change was inevitable.[82]

Calling on contacts from his previous position, Bowlin met in 2001 with Graham MacKay of South African Breweries (SAB) to discuss the world beer market. MacKay brought up the idea of purchasing Miller. The eventual deal was announced on May 30, 2002, in an acquisition totaling $5.6 billion and with Norman Adami as new CEO in 2003. Adami was an experienced beer man, with nine years managing SAB's Johannesburg brewery. Over the next three years, Adami ended a fifteen-year decline in sales. By 2004, sales of Miller Lite accounted for 40 percent of the brewer's approximately $5 billion in sales and rose 12.5 percent by volume. Despite aggressive price cuts by Anheuser-Busch in 2005, Miller Lite still grew 3.2 percent, compared with flat growth for Bud Light and a dip for the industry overall. Adami helped knock Anheuser off its pedestal. In 2005, Anheuser's operating income fell 22 percent, to $2.6 billion, its first such decline in about ten years. Domestic volume flopped 1.8 percent, to 101 million barrels.[83]

Graham MacKay, the chief executive of SABMiller, earned a degree in engineering from the University of Witwatersrand in 1972 and a commerce degree from the University of South Africa in 1977. He joined SAB Ltd. in 1978 as a systems manager and served in a number of senior positions, including chairman and group managing director. He became chief executive of South African Breweries when it was listed on the London Stock Exchange in 1999. *Photo courtesy of Miller/Coors.*

Adami moved on to a broader SABMiller role and was replaced by Tom Long, who had joined Miller Brewing Company in 2005 after seventeen years at Coca-Cola Company. Long eventually served as global vice-president and director of strategic marketing and vice-president of national sales in the United States.

In 2008, SABMiller and Molson Coors entered into a joint venture to create MillerCoors and moved the firm's headquarters, and 375 jobs, to Chicago. After the merger, Leo Kiely was chief executive officer for MillerCoors following an extensive stint as president and chief executive officer of Molson Coors Brewing Company. He retired in 2011 and was replaced by Long. In 2010, the firm launched its Tenth and Blake Beer Company to focus on craft and import beers, and by 2011, MillerCoors operated eight major breweries in the United States, as well several smaller microbreweries, including Leinenkugel's Tenth Street Brewery in Milwaukee.[84]

Blatz Brewing Company

Blatz Brewing was founded by John (Johann) Braun in 1846, originally called the City Brewery. Initially, Braun produced about 150 barrels of beer annually until 1851, when Valentine Blatz, a former employee who was trained in the brewing arts in Bavaria, established his own brewery adjacent to Braun's plant.

Braun was killed in an accident later that year, and Blatz quickly married his neighbor's widow, thereby uniting the City Brewery and his own operation.[85] The arrangement was just one more demonstration that in Milwaukee, love, beer and business can go easily hand in hand.

When the couple married, the combined breweries produced only 350 barrels per year. However, by 1880, total annual production had reached 125,000 barrels. The brewery's growth continued, and in 1884, Blatz ranked as the third-largest beer producer in Milwaukee.

Blatz was the first Milwaukee brewer to market beer nationally, with distribution centers in Chicago, New York, Boston, New Orleans, Memphis, Charleston and Savannah. He was also the first of the Milwaukee brewers to include a bottling plant within his brewery. A canny businessman who realized that he often didn't need a middleman, Blatz had his own carpenter shop, cooperage, machine shop and coal yard, as well as his own railroad cars to haul product to his far-reaching empire.[86]

In 1890, Blatz sold his brewery to several overseas investors, known as the English Syndicate, who managed the plant until Prohibition, when it began making chewing gum and soda. Following repeal of the Eighteenth Amendment in 1933, Blatz was issued federal permit No. WIS-U-712, allowing it to again brew beer. Schenley Industries, a New York–based whiskey producer, snapped up Blatz, along with brands from many companies that went out of business in the 1930s.[87] The company regained its fans and again did well, producing more than 1 million barrels annually during the halcyon 1940s and 1950s. Among its numerous labels at that time were Blatz, Pilsener, Old Heidelberg, Private Stock, Milwaukee Dark, Culmbacher, Continental Special, Tempo and English Style Ale. In 1955, Schenley ranked 182 on the Fortune 500 list when it still held the Blatz name in its portfolio.[88]

By then, competition had edged out Blatz as a major brewing player. Soaring manufacturing expenses limited its growth. Subsequently, in 1958, Schenley sold the brewery name to Pabst. Yet in a legal quirk, a federal court order prevented Pabst from brewing at Blatz facilities in Milwaukee. In 1959, Blatz ceased all operations, and Pabst purchased all the Blatz brands. It re-launched the brand as a craft-style beer. In 1969, the G. Heileman Brewing Company of La Crosse purchased Blatz from Pabst after an antitrust lawsuit.

But in 1996, the Stroh Brewery of Detroit bought out Heileman in bankruptcy court and, in effect, owned Blatz. In another quirk of history, in 1999, Pabst acquired most of Stroh's holdings, including Blatz. Pabst, now a virtual brewer, does not own any plants but contracts with MillerCoors to handle Pabst production—and, once again, the famous Blatz beers.[89]

Many of the company's former offices and production facilities have been taken over by private developers for condominiums and offices, as well as by the Milwaukee School of Engineering. The German Renaissance limestone and brick buildings, 1101–47 North Broadway, were listed on the National Register of Historic Places on April 15, 1986.[90]

Gettelman Brewing Company

At first glance, Adam Gettelman may seem an anomaly as a Milwaukee brewer. He was one of the few Milwaukee business leaders in a profession usually headed by German immigrants. But his European heritage was close enough. Gettelman was born on April 27, 1847, in Germantown, Wisconsin, just north of Milwaukee. His farmer father, Peter Gettelmann [sic] was a German émigré, as was his mother, Catherine Holl. Her father, Jacob, had fought in the Napoleonic Wars and was stranded in Russia with the collapse of the French army in 1812. He managed to make his way back home to his home state of Hesse and came to America with his family in 1837. Later in life, Adam Gettelman dropped the second "n" in the family name.

Nancy Moore Gettelman, in her rollicking good history about the family's business, relates that young Adam Gettelman had no inclination to be a farmer but instead went to the John Ennis Brewing School in Milwaukee. He then apprenticed at the Menominee Brewing Company, owned by George Schweickhart. The latter was a native of Muhlhausen, Alsace, a village on the French-German border, and descended from a long line of beer makers. Schweickhart came to America in 1833 and started his own operation on the old Watertown Plank Road, not far from the Menominee River, valued for its fresh, clear water. Nearby farms provided barley and hops, with stone from adjacent quarries used for the brew house and related buildings. At the time, there were fifteen other breweries in Milwaukee, with beer selling for a

Right: Adam Gettelman. *Photo courtesy of Nancy Moore Gettelman.*

Below: The A. Gettelman Brewery is visible in the distance as a group of buildings on the right side of the road. Miller Brewing Company's complex is in the foreground in this photo from the 1860s. *Photo courtesy of Nancy Moore Gettelman.*

dollar a barrel. Schweickhart produced about fifteen hundred barrels a year and needed help to expand. So the hardworking young Gettelman was an appreciated addition to the company's workforce and worked his way up in the corporate ladder.

Like many single fellows of his day, Gettelman cast an appreciative eye on the boss's daughter. On November 24, 1870, he married Magdalena Schweickhart and eventually sired eight children, six of whom survived. In 1871, Magdalena's father sold an interest in his firm, now called Schweickhart Brewery, to his new son-in-law. In 1874, he sold another share to a second son-in-law, Charles Schuckmann, who was a partner in a successful wine and liquor-wholesaling firm launched in 1857, located at 409 Chestnut Street in Milwaukee.[91] Gettelman bought out Schuckmann and took over total control of the brewery in 1876. A fire in 1877 heavily damaged the brewery, to the tune of $31,550. Gettelman sent a check for $100 to Milwaukee fire chief Henry Lippert, thanking him and his men "as an acknowledgment of the timely service." The chief subsequently placed the check in the Firemen's Benevolent Fund.[92]

The company quickly expanded at its facilities on Forty-fourth and State Streets in Milwaukee, not far from the Miller Brewing Company. In 1891, the brewery offered $1,000 to anyone who could prove Gettelman Beer contained any substitute for pure malt and hops. The reward went unclaimed for eighty years, until the last batch of Gettelman rolled off the line. But in 2007, the first new offering of the Gettelman brand since 1971 was tapped at a ceremony in the Miller Brewing Company Visitor Center. A single keg was produced by Miller brewmaster David Ryder, according to a Gettelman family recipe. All those present, among them members of the Gettelman family, approved of the brew. There were no takers on that long-ago challenge.[93]

In 1898, Gettelman and Fred Miller, as presidents of their respective breweries, jointly asked for Milwaukee's assistance in getting city water to their plants, which were only blocks from each other. Permission was granted. During Prohibition, Gettelman wisely sought alternatives to making beer and invested in gold mining and a sugar beet factory. He also remained president of the West Side Bank, which he had founded in 1894. When Gettelman died in 1925, his son, William, took over the presidency until 1929, when he assumed control of his late father's bank. Succeeding William was his brother, Frederick, nicknamed "Fritz." The new boss understood the business inside and out, having worked in the brewery's bottlehouse, boiler room, lab, malt house and cooperage. Fritz had also attended the

Above: A full load of Gettelman beer barrels is pulled by two strong draft horses. Depending on the route and the steepness of hills, some loads needed six to eight animals. *Photo courtesy of Nancy Moore Gettelman.*

Below: Gettelman employees and delivery wagons are ready for work, poised outside the brewery's Victorian buildings in the 1880s. *Photo courtesy of Nancy Moore Gettelman.*

Gettelman's brewery. *Photo courtesy of Nancy Moore Gettelman.*

Wahl-Henius Brewing Institute in Chicago and graduated as a certified brewmaster. At age twenty-two, he was his father's chief assistant, being in charge of all brewery operations. After Prohibition, Fritz led the brewery's acquisition of thirty-five taverns around Milwaukee and regularly stopped at each to have a drink with their patrons and check on the business. A true character, Fritz also smoked a box of cigars a day and drove on his rounds behind the wheel of his Packard, accompanied by his trusty spaniel, Rex.

Fritz was also an avid engineer, inventing a pasteurizing device and the first successful steel beer keg, a handy substitute for the old wooden barrel. The new containers were soon being produced by Milwaukee's A.O. Smith Company, based on drawings that Gettelman had quickly sketched out.[94] He then went on to develop a line of beer cans for the American Can Company. Always promotions-oriented, Gettelman was Milwaukee's first brewer to advertise on television, hosting wrestling matches at the Eagles Club as early as 1947. On many multistory wall paintings, the company's mascot, Fritzie, was often featured in funny predicaments, cartoons that drew laughs as well as customers.

Fritz Gettelman loved his desk in the A. Gettelman Brewery's old office, instead of the "new" building constructed in 1948. A light bulb made in Holland hung above his desk, burning night and day for more than thirty years. *Photo courtesy of Nancy Moore Gettelman.*

Fritz Gettelman was joined by his sons Fred Jr. and Tom, both of whom edged into management and were in good positions to assume leadership roles when the elder Gettelman died on June 23, 1954. Continuing his father's penchant for tinkering, Tom Gettelman devised a device for easily carrying the company's signature cone-shaped cans, coining the market slogan "Pik-Up-Six." Led by the brothers, the firm expanded into Chicago, Boston and other cities in the late 1950s, despite the financial challenges of surviving a seventy-six-day brewery workers' strike in 1953 that affected all of Milwaukee's breweries.

By the 1960s, however, Tom and Fred Jr. had decided to sell their again-thriving business and spoke with Norman Klug, president of neighboring Miller Brewing, about their plans. Miller was in expansion mode at the time, and the two longtime brewing neighbors concluded a mutually satisfactory deal in 1961.[95] The Gettelman brand has remained with Miller ever since.

3

A Shot and a Beer

Good fresh beer is unquestionably beneficial.
—Milwaukee Sentinel, *July 29, 1879*

What goes around comes around. Especially when it pertains to Milwaukee's brewing scene. In the early 1800s, numerous taverns and restaurants produced their own froth, often in the basement cellar to be hauled upstairs to slake the thirst of discerning patrons. As these entrepreneurs expanded operations, they built larger facilities, hired more workers and developed marketing programs, and *ein prosit!*, Miller, Pabst, Schlitz, Blatz, Gettelman and other brands were everywhere drinkers gathered.

It's no different today, and small breweries and brewpubs proliferate as drinkers hone their tastes and seek something above and beyond the commercial beers.

SPRECHER BREWING COMPANY

When Randy Sprecher launched his brewery in 1985, few drinkers around Milwaukee really knew much about microbrews. Sprecher was the first to start up such a small brewery after Prohibition punched out the lights on Milwaukee's beer and spirits industry. It's a different world now, particularly when Sprecher's operation continues to pull in awards, including eight top medals at the 2010 Los Angeles International Beer Competition.

Sprecher also won two gold, five silver and one bronze medal at the 2010 United States Open Beer Championships, making it the second-highest-placing brewer in a competition of twenty international breweries and award-winning home-brewers. The awards list continues: in 2004, the firm was named the Great American Beer Festival's Small Brewing Company and Small Brewing Company Brewmaster of the Year, the same year that Milwaukee's own Miller Brewing Company was named top-ranked Large Brewing Company.

The firm presents one of the heftiest lineups of beers in the region, ranging from Russian Imperial Stout to an India Pale Ale once favored by British troops on the subcontinent. It also produces enough seasonals to overflow a beer wagon.

Sprecher was a home-brewer since 1971, starting while in physical oceanography school at what is now called California State University at Humboldt. He had first discovered how good beers could taste while serving with the army in Germany. In 1980, after taking fermentation science at the University of California–Davis, Sprecher moved to Milwaukee after being recruited by Pabst Brewing Company as a supervisor. Sprecher's job at Pabst came after an interview while attending university; this, combined with his age, family and military experience, seemed to be important to the brewery management at the time.

He was hired by the late Karl Strauss, longtime vice-president of production. Sprecher's knowledge of home-brewing did not seem to be a factor in landing his job, but at least his basic background in knowing the brewing process was a help. Sprecher was sent directly to the brew house, spending four years there and then in other parts of the plant, receiving on-the-job training from the malt house to packaging. Sprecher learned the most in the yeast room, since culture collection and control are paramount to any brewing operation. He credited Pabst's corporate guy in control of all cultures, John Brazin, for sharing his extensive knowledge of the brewmaking process.

While at Pabst, Sprecher still found time and interest in brewing new recipes at home. The workers started calling him "California Dreamer" because he was telling them that some day he was going to build his own brewery. When Sprecher was laid off from Pabst, he pursued his dream of having his own facility.

Finding an existing site was a challenge, so Sprecher designed and built his first place with $40,000 cash at the former Pfister & Vogel tannery

A Shot and a Beer

Randy Sprecher, of the award-winning Sprecher Brewery, hoists one of his brews. When he launched his operation in 1985, Sprecher was the first entrepreneur to start up a small brewery in Milwaukee since Prohibition. *Photo courtesy of Sprecher Brewery.*

complex south of downtown Milwaukee, at 710 West Oregon Street. The original space was about 5,000 square feet, with another 5,000 available in the basement. The office areas covered about 400 square feet per floor for a total of about 11,200 for the building. In 1995, Sprecher Brewing moved to 701 West Glendale Avenue, to a space that was about three times the size of the brewery's first location.[1]

Sprecher selected his first commercial brews based on his personal homebrewing list. Black Bavarian was the initial beverage, followed by Special Amber. For Sprecher, a good beer is one with drinkability, with Milwaukee beer so special because of the quality of Lake Michigan water, along with his beverages' balance, drinkability and extensive diversity in the product line. Sprecher now produces fifteen thousand barrels of beer a year, with the most popular being the long-running Special Amber and Black Bavarian, followed by Oktoberfest and Mai Bock, with Abbey Triple gaining quickly.

As with any manufacturer, Sprecher keeps inventing new brews to keep up with the always-expanding market, as well as incrementally changing some brands for continued improvement. Since 1979, the firm has been active in the Master Brewers Association of the Americas. In 2010–11, Sprecher's

president, Jeff Hamilton, was also president of the Wisconsin Brewers Guild. Hamilton, who had been vice-president and general manager since 2005, became Sprecher president in February 2010. Sprecher himself retained the title of chief executive officer, with his wife, Anne, as manager of communications and marketing.

Chameleon Brewing Company, a Sprecher offshoot, brews several craft beers, including an American pale ale called Hop on Hop, along with Fire Light, Wiffy and an India Pale Ale/ rye hybrid. Its first bottles came out in January 2010, with the company name representing the changing age in brewing.[2]

As with most brewers, Sprecher likes his beer, favoring his Black Bavarian year round and others based on weather and mood. His new fun is developing the newer markets that find Sprecher beer to their liking, particularly on the West Coast, where the brewer now lives part of the year. In 2010, the firm celebrated its twenty-fifth anniversary with an on-site release of Sprecher's limited edition Kriek (cherry) Lambic, made with Wisconsin organic malt and Door County cherry juice. Festivities included an open house, tours, ping-pong, root beer float drinking and

Black Bavarian, Dunkel Weizen and Winter Brew were among Sprecher Brewery's first offerings. *Photos courtesy of Sprecher Brewery.*

brat eating contests, a deejay, dachshund races and a competition for the Most Authentic German Costume and one for a Randy Sprecher look-alike. Music was by the Rabid Aardvarks, a local band noted for its contemporary pop, rock and modern country sounds.

The company remains one of the most promotions-minded breweries in the area. It regularly hosts appearances by personalities such as 2010 Mid-American Stock Car Series Champion Lyle Nowak signing autographs and swapping stories about life in the fast lane. It also works with the Wisconsin Beef Council on the Grilling with Beer competition at the Wisconsin State Fair. By 2011, the firm had created Sprecher Beer Flavored Kettle Chips, out just in time for the Green Bay Packers to win the Super Bowl.[3]

Ever alert to trends, noting that many outside events were cutting back on use of glass bottles, Sprecher began selling its popular Special Amber brand in cans in the spring of 2011. The firm thus joined a growing list of other Wisconsin craft breweries also seeking to slash packaging and delivery costs by using the aluminum cans.[4]

LAKEFRONT BREWING COMPANY

Launched in 1987 by brothers Jim and Russ Klisch, Lakefront Brewing Company produces a great range of beers from its home in the former Milwaukee Electric Railway and Light Company power plant. The sprawling brick facility at 1872 North Commerce Street is on the west bank of the Milwaukee River, just north of downtown Milwaukee. Along with its signature Riverwest Stein that makes up some 25 percent of production, the brewery makes numerous award-winning beverages, including Wheat Monkey, Cream City Pale Ale, Fuel Café Coffee Stout and an India Pale Ale. Its lagers include East Side Dark and Klisch Pilsner, as well as a wide variety of seasonals. Among the latter is a Pumpkin Lager, which is also made into pumpkin vodka in conjunction with Great Lakes Distillery, as well as the "Pure Milwaukee Genius Series," with a special reserve and American Red Ale, among others.

In 1981, Jim Klisch expressed interest in beer making, so his brother, Russ, humored him by giving him a book on the subject for his August 22 birthday that year. Jim subsequently read the book and brewed his first beer. Taking up a sibling challenge, Russ also began brewing. They both began entering home-brewing competitions and won several awards. With this success, their family and friends encouraged them to turn their hobby into a business.

Jim and Russ Klisch founded Lakefront Brewery in 1987. Their beers have won numerous awards, and the brewery is the first in the state and the first business in the city of Milwaukee to receive the Travel Green Wisconsin certification. *Photo by Darlene Carlson.*

It helped that there were family roots in the beer industry. The Klisches' grandfather, George Solberg, worked for Jos. Schlitz Brewing Co., driving a delivery truck. Solberg brought home short fills for their dad, Joe, who had earlier owned the fabled Nightingale Bar. Several other family members were also in the tavern business. In rustic Thorp, Wisconsin, Jim Klische's godfather owned a tavern called Leon & Lils', doing a rip-roaring business for fifty years. A great-aunt also owned a tavern.

With that family history and their common interest in beer making, the brothers launched their operations, wisely starting small. From home, they could walk to their first brewery, a sixty- by sixty-foot space in a refurbished bakery building at 818 East Chambers Street. Starting inexpensively, the brothers' initial equipment consisted of several stainless steel fifty-five-gallon drums and used dairy equipment. They cobbled together bits and pieces of equipment, causing Russ to call it the "Frankenstein brewery." Finally, on December 2, 1987, they sold their first barrel of beer at the funky, kickback Gordon Park Pub. Now called Nessun Dorma, the upscale watering hole still sells Lakefront's beer.[5]

As Lakefront Brewery's popularity exploded, so did production. By 1988, sales jumped to seventy-two barrels; by 1989, it totaled 125 barrels, with sales beginning to double after that. By 1998, the production reached almost three thousand barrels, so Lakefront began scouring Milwaukee for expanded space.

The search led them to their current building, a classic Cream City brick building dating from 1908. As part of its past life, the building was sold to the City of Milwaukee for its Forestry Department. In 1999, Milwaukee restaurateur Russ Davis, who was interested in opening an eatery in the brewery's large hall, approached the brothers. Subsequently, the team launched the Lakefront Brewery Palm Garden, which is noted for its boisterous Friday fish fry year round, attracting hundreds of diners who are seated together at large tables. Reservations are accepted for groups of eight or more before 5:30 p.m. for people seeking a traditional Milwaukee fish fry with a selection of the brewery's fine beers on draft. The Brewhaus Polka Kings add an extra Germanic touch to the evenings festivities. The vast party space is also regularly used for private events ranging from political rallies to weddings.

The lights in the Palm Garden were originally designed in 1916 and hung in the Plankinton House Hotel, a massive sandstone palace in downtown Milwaukee built by meatpacker John Plankinton. The hotel never used the room for its originally intended purpose as a beer hall because Prohibition laws were passed. So the space became a restaurant, with the lights hanging there until 1982, when the building was demolished. The City of Milwaukee stored the chandeliers in a warehouse until the Klisch brothers placed a winning bid on them at an auction. It was an expensive undertaking to restore the lights to their original condition.

The brothers added an original German-made copper brew house to their riverfront complex in 2000, helping boost production to 6,292 barrels brewed in 2005 and up to 8,863 barrels in 2006. By 2008, production hit 11,000 barrels.

Lakefront Brewery has several firsts to its credit. It was the first Milwaukee beer company to bottle fruit beer since Prohibition, starting in 1992 with a seasonal Lakefront Cherry Beer. The beer was created with an old home-brewing recipe and the Klisches' penchant for Door County cherries. The brewery was the first certified organic brewery to produce organic beer under its own label in the United States, beginning in 1996 with its Lakefront Organic ESB (extra special bitter), which uses Wisconsin-grown organic malt and ORGANIC hops shipped in from New Zealand. The brewery also produces an award-winning gluten-free beer called New Grist, brewed from sorghum, hops, water, rice and gluten-free yeast grown on molasses.[6]

In May 2007, the Wisconsin Department of Tourism named Lakefront Brewery the first brewery in the state and the first business in the city of Milwaukee to receive the Travel Green Wisconsin certification. The award recognizes tourism-related businesses working to reduce their environmental impact. Lakefront donates approximately fifteen thousand pounds of spent grain each week to Growing Power, a nonprofit organization based in Milwaukee that provides healthy, nutrient-rich produce to inner-city markets and to restaurants throughout the Midwest.[7] For an additional business coup, the brewery is Milwaukee's first microbrewery to achieve Regional Craft Brewery status.[8]

Klisches' philosophy is that visitors go on brewery tours for three main reasons: "to drink beer, be entertained and see the place." Capitalizing on these factors, the company offers beer at the start of the tour, then shares jokes along the way and still manages to explain the brewing process and Lakefront's history.

Lakefront also owns Bernie Brewer's Chalet, once part of the old Milwaukee County Stadium, home of the Milwaukee Brewers. In 1973, Bernie began celebrating home runs by stepping out of his chalet and sliding into a frothy beer mug, then releasing balloons. When the team rebuilt its stadium in 2001, the newly named Miller Park needed another "house" for its mascot, so the Klisches bought the original one for $18,000 and shows it off during his brewery tours.[9]

For the Klisches, in the last twenty to thirty years, the customer has become better educated about the different craft beer styles. The desire of Americans in general to want more taste, flavor and variety in all their foods, including beer, and the amount of different ingredients that are available to craft brewers to create innovative, tasty styles of beer have caused the craft beer market to grow in double digits.[10] The brewery employs twenty full-time and twenty part-time staff, distributing to thirty-five states. From a meager production from the fifty-five-gallon drums that started in 1987, Lakefront brewed 17,641 barrels in 2010.[11]

Brew House Pubs

Hard on the heels of the micro and craft brewers have been the brew house pubs in Milwaukee, again following the grand tradition of saloonkeepers often making their own beers.

Since 1987 Water Street Brewery, has been a fixture on Milwaukee's trendy lower East Side bar 'hood, then opening in Delafield in 1999 and in Grafton along the I-43 corridor in 2010. Water Street Brewery, located at 1101 North Water Street, offers a honey lager, Bavarian and raspberry weiss, pale ale and the always-fabulous Water Street Amber for a nod to its original site. The Water Street locale is packed with a wide range of brewery memorabilia, from beer trays to tappers.[12]

Taking over the century-old Saddlery Building in the Third Ward in 1997, the Milwaukee Ale House at 233 North Water Street is one of the granddaddies of the city's microbrewing scene. Owner Jim McCabe's fresh beers capitalize on Milwaukee's heritage, with the Solomon Juneau Extra Pale Ale (EPA), Louie's Demise Amber, Pull Chain Pail Ale, the robust Sheepshead Irish-style Stout and Ulao, a straw-colored Belgian punched up with hints of ginger, orange peel and cracked coriander. It also serves several seasonals. In addition to its beer selection, the Ale House is noted for its music scene and restaurant, with views overlooking the Milwaukee River. Its parent firm, the Milwaukee Brewing Company, provides beer products to the Milwaukee County Department of Parks, Recreation and Culture. As part of a "green exchange," the brewery takes the county's vegetable oil and uses it in its biodiesel generator. Subsequently, the oil from the parks' fish fries goes to power the equipment in the brewery to make the beer the county sells.[13]

The Horny Goat Hideaway/Brewing Company has one of the largest outdoor patios in the Milwaukee area, perfect for views of the Kinnickinnic River. Opened in 2009 by Jim Sorenson, the brewpub offered several popular labels made under contract with the Stevens Point Brewery. The selections included Exposed, a light-colored, farmhouse-style ale brewed with wheat, oats and malted barley, and Hopped Up 'n' Horny, an American pale ale with a great malt bite. The Goat also produced a Belgian witbier, accented by orange peel. The Horny Blonde was a light-bodied lager, while the Horny Goat Red Vixen presented a reddish-amber hue and a foamy head. Its Stacked Milk Stout was made as a traditional English stout that was creamier than an Irish stout. Among the brewery's seasonal presentations was a Munich-style Octoberfest amber and the Nutcracker, similar to a Bavarian wheat bock.[14]

After launching its first brews in November 2010, Jeff Garwood's Big Bay Brewing opened its tasting room at 4517 North Oakland Avenue in Shorewood, a North Shore–Milwaukee suburb. The brewery held a grand opening on March 20, 2011, to coincide with the spring equinox. Fans of the

A Shot and a Beer

Above: Jim Sorenson, owner, Horny Goat Hideaway/Brewing Company *Photo by Darlene Carlson.*

Opposite page:
Top: The Milwaukee Ale House in Milwaukee's trendy Old Third Ward district opened in 1997 as one of the city's first brew house pubs. *Photo by Darlene Carlson.*
Middle: Jim McCabe of the Milwaukee Ale House. *Photo by Darlene Carlson.*
Bottom: The Milwaukee Ale House is located in Milwaukee's historic Saddlery Building at 233 North Water Street in the Third Ward. *Photo by Darlene Carlson.*

brewery's Boatilla Amber Ale and Wavehopper could then purchase the beer at the critically reviewed North Star Bistro across Oakland and at many Sendik's grocery store outlets, as well as at area liquor stores such as Otto's Wine & Spirits. In February 2011, the Three Lions British pub opened in the building just south of Big Bay's facilities and continues to serve the brewery's beers. Big Bay is brewed under license with the Milwaukee Brewing Company.[15]

St. Francis Brewery and Restaurant at 3825 South Kinnickinnic Avenue in St Francis has a mellow golden ale with a smooth crisp taste; a Bohemian-style pilsner; a filtered amber ale dazzled with four different styles of hops; and an English-inspired, medium-bodied nut brown ale. Hearty drinkers love the brewmaster Scott Hettig's oatmeal stout, which is still surprisingly light despite its chocolately flavor, while his weissbier is made in the traditional Bavarian mode, with banana and clove flavors for that special punch.[16]

One can hardly get any more local than Stonefly Brewing Company, located at 735 West Center Street in Milwaukee's cozy Riverwest neighborhood. The labels alone are worth a try: Mustache Ride Pale Ale, Six-Finger IAP, Four Wolves English Ale, Brass Knuckle Blonde, Brewtown Brown, Pierce Street Port, an oatmeal stout and Simon Bagley Stout. "Make beer, not war," is the company's common sense suggestion. The firm, originally Paul Onopa's Onopa Brewery, was purchased by Julia LaLoggia and Rose Billingsley in 2004, when Onopa retired.[17]

4

Bottoms Up

Milwaukee Distilling

When it's ready, it's ready.
—*Guy Rehorst, Great Lakes Distillery*[1]

Here's a toast to the late, lamented spirits producers who once made Milwaukee really famous. Gone are Emil Kiewert, John Hrobsky, Emil Bloch, H. Van Emden, Joseph Duester, Bade & Warnken and Lakeside Distilling. Alas, there are no more pours of Joseph Dudenhoefer's Pater Oschwald and his Sunny Castle Rye or of Peter Barth's Blue Bell Rye Whiskey. Also long gone is La Belle Whiskey, made by A. Breslauer & Co.; K. Andrzejewski's Club Whiskey; Davy Crockett Whiskey, produced by Zacher & Jensen; and those cheerful glasses of Red Seal Rye from Newman & Frisch.[2]

At one time, however, distilleries were as much a part of Milwaukee's burgeoning business scene as the breweries. With the rush of new immigrants into Milwaukee prior to the Civil War, distilling boomed. The newcomers' "turrible tirst" was readily slaked in those days when potent beverages sold for a mere fifteen cents a gallon. Some of Milwaukee's earliest distilleries did not only make liquor but ale and beer as well. The first was what became the Lake Brewery, now the site of the Milwaukee County Transit bus garage.[3]

Among Milwaukee's earliest distillers was Thomas O'Neill, who was born in Dublin in 1821 and came to America in 1832. He moved to Milwaukee from the East Coast in 1844 and began farming. As a sideline, he established the Pleasant Springs Distillery in 1860 in the village of Greenfield, just south of Milwaukee. O'Neill moved the spirits operation to the town of Lake in 1864. In 1858, O'Neill married Margaretta Reynolds, and the couple bore three sons. John, the oldest, was in charge of the distillery. O'Neill was elected to the Wisconsin Assembly in 1875 and was a town clerk.[1]

Another early distillery was the John P. Kissinger Company, which was launched in 1856 and lasted until 1918. The company produced Arbutus, Harvester Bourbon, Monadnock Rye, Old Veteran, Unexcelled, Velvet Finish and Washita Rye. Located variously at 85 Keel (1863), 155 Reed (1865–66) and 278 East Water (1867–1918), the firm's names leapfrogged from John P. Kissinger (1863–66), to J.P. Kissinger & Co. (1867), then back to John P. Kissinger (1868–75) and finally returning to J.P. Kissinger & Co. (1877–1918).[5]

The federal government, ever on the lookout for a taxing opportunity nationwide when the Civil War broke out, set a dollar-a-barrel tax on beer and a dollar-a-gallon tax on whiskey. Under the two administrations of hearty drinker President Ulysses Grant, between 1869 and 1877, the whiskey tax was elevated to a lofty two dollars a gallon. Although there was the typical widespread mumbling about such fees, these regulations actually didn't hamper Wisconsin's distilling business. Immediately after the war, the largest Milwaukee-area distillers included Otto Bierbach (1866–68), Brunst & Casperi, Koeffler Bros. (1866–67), O'Neill & Reynolds (1871–78), RindsKopf & Son (1863–70), J.B. Schram, P. Young (1866) and the multi-named Schuckmann & Waldeck (1862–74), which morphed into Waldeck & Seligmann (1875) and then Schuckmann & Seligmann (1877–1911), producing the potent Eremite, Maryland Club and Prince William whiskeys.[6]

But there was a cloud on the drinking horizon. Ever the competitors, Chicago distillers entered the Wisconsin market with gusto, seeing a ripe market for cheap drink. The flatlanders peddled their whiskey in Milwaukee for $1.15 a gallon, raising eyebrows among the locals, who figured that if the Chicagoans could sell cut-rate whiskey supposedly taxed at $2.00, then somebody wasn't paying the feds their due. Or they were paying off the tax collectors. Eventually, even the Milwaukee distillers were cutting the same corners.

In 1876, Congress decided that a manufacturer of contraband booze would be sent to jail, as well as slapped with a hefty fine. At least one Milwaukee distiller, Jacob Nunnemacher, figured it was time to try another line of work rather than be fined or sent to jail. He subsequently sold his Nunnemacher Distillery in the town of Lake to the Kinnickinnic Distilling Company at 54 Oneida Street (1870–73). Kinnickinnic Distilling closed after a few short years, leaving only Meadow Springs Distilling Co., Wm. Bergenthal Co. and John Meiner Distillery as major players in the industry.[7]

Meadow Springs has one of the more interesting histories. On a blustery December 4, 1882, Leopold Wirth, Gustav Niemeier and Henry Koch Jr. filed articles of incorporation for what was to be Meadow Springs Distillery. The *Daily Republican-Sentinel* newspaper said that "the business of the organization is implied in its name" and that the new firm's capital stock was pegged at $30,000.

Wirth, Koch and Niemeier were not any different from other entrepreneurs of their era, especially with alcohol production being one of the city's growth trades. In 1882, Milwaukee's breweries brought in $8 million net in revenue, and distilleries did a fabulous $4.5 million in profits. Not much is known about Niemeier, except that he was a passenger agent for the Hamburg & Bremen Steamship Company and a freight dealer for the Baltimore & Ohio Railroad. Partner Koch was born in Germany in 1849 and came to Milwaukee in 1854 with his parents. His father set up a cooperage, and young Koch learned the trade in the family's Mill Street plant. Koch had also been elected alderman in 1880, serving one term.

Wirth was a popular character around Milwaukee since he dealt in furs, horses, skins and other wholesale goods. He worked for a time with Hartman & Company liquor dealers. One of Wirth's more lucrative sidelines was buying skinny cattle and fattening them up with spent grain, the leftover mash residue purchased from the city's distilleries and breweries. The herds were then sold at a profit. With this background, Wirth convinced his pals to cut out the middleman in the cattle dealings, suggesting that setting up their own distillery would provide these grains for the cattle. Value added, so to speak.

On January 10, 1883, the three sat down in one of the top "ladies and gents restaurants" in Milwaukee and held their first stockholders' meeting. The session was held at the elegant Miller & Holtz's at the corner of

Leopold Wirth, Meadow Springs Distillery. *Photo courtesy of Sensient Technologies.*

Above, left: Adolph Zinn, Meadow Springs Distillery. *Photo courtesy of Sensient Technologies.*

Above, right: William Bergenthal, Wm. Bergenthal Company. *Photo courtesy of Sensient Technologies.*

Grand Avenue and North Water Street. That day was marred, however, when a fire broke out around the corner in the Newhall House hotel, killing between sixty and eighty persons. The exact figure was not known because the guest register was destroyed in the blaze. Numerous guests and staff leapt to their deaths from upper windows, crashing onto the ice-crusted sidewalks several stories below. Niemeier's office was also located in the Newhall and was gutted in the fire. But despite the chaos outside, the meeting continued, with Wirth elected Meadow Springs' president, Niemeier vice-president and Koch secretary-treasurer.

Among the company's underwriters was Adolph C. Zinn, owner of the Milwaukee Malt House. Zinn was born a wagonmaker's son in 1849 in Saxony. Since he realized that Meadow Springs needed a manager with distilling know-how, he hired William Bergenthal, a hardworking Westphalian who came to Milwaukee in 1867. Successful in a number of businesses, Bergenthal owned the Wm. Bergenthal Company, a distillery and liquor producer located at 476 and 478 Fourth Street, a large building on the corner of Cherry Street. His annual salary at Meadow Springs was pegged at $1,500.

Meadow Springs' first barrel of whiskey was sold on July 5, 1883, with production at Bergenthal's own facility, an imposing complex along the Milwaukee River about five miles north of Milwaukee's downtown. Bergenthal also made compressed yeast, turning out about one thousand pounds of product a day and shipping much of it to St. Louis and Chicago. Basically, Bergenthal was a spirits man, with his firm producing bourbon, malt whiskeys, gin, brandies, rum and cordials, and he also imported wine, champagne and cognac. Among his labels were Old Lexington, Mohawk, W.H. McBrayer, Hermitage, Old Crow, Bond and Lillard, OFC, M.V. Monarch, R. Monarch, Anderson, Anderson Country Sour Mash, T.B. Ripy, Henry Clay (J.E. Pepper & Co.), Ashland, Mellwood, Blue Grass, Guckenheimer, Montrose and Overholt.[8]

The Bergenthal operations were described in media of the day as

> *a two-story structure with basement having vaults and sub-cellars thirty feet below. They are the largest and most complete in the Northwest, and are only adapted for the storage of wines, foreign and native, and for preserving them in all seasons at a certain required temperature. In these splendid vaults, so far removed from adverse influences are kept the best vintages of fine old imported and native wines in casks.*
>
> *Ample means for through ventilation have been provided and these superior beverages are kept in the most perfect condition and shipped to consumers in all parts, who are invariably pleased with their high quality. On the ground and upper floors are also stored a splendid stock of old bourbon and rye whiskies, known as the leading brands of American gins, brandies, rums, and cordials. The basement is devoted to the storage of ales, porters, and mineral waters, and case goods of Rhine and Moselle wines, Clarets, Burgundies, and different other kinds imported in glass.*
>
> *On the first floor are the offices and the stock, operating and packing rooms, while the second floor is used for surplus goods. The company are direct importers of the best French, German, Russian, Norwegian, and English productions and their trade extends over Wisconsin, Michigan, Illinois, Minnesota, Iowa, Nebraska, Utah, Washington, Oregon and the two Dakotas. Twelve capable assistants are employed in the house and six traveling salesmen are kept continually upon the road.*

Bergenthal's top aide was the German-born Henry Figge, whose connection with the house as a traveling salesman dated from 1876.[9]

Bergenthal was noted for his temper. Once he and his younger brother, August, threw out a tax-collecting deputy sheriff from their office after the man made some derogatory comments about the Bergenthal company's

By the 1880s, Meadow Springs Distillery was already expanding its plant in the Menomonee Valley. *Photo courtesy of Sensient Technologies.*

operations. Apparently, the fellow was referring to an incident in the early 1870s, when young Augie and his partner, John Schlitz, spent four months in the county jail for allegedly misrepresenting the company's alcohol tax records. However, the *Milwaukee Sentinel* reported that the two young men had so many visitors to the cell that the sheriff had to specify days "of public reception in order that his business may not suffer by the tramp, tramp, tramp of the friends of the prisoners." When August married the lovely Appolina Klaus in 1878, one of his groomsmen was Charles Grau, who would later become a major stockholder in Meadow Springs.

Red Star Yeast's first delivery wagon was pulled by a lone horse. *Photo courtesy of Sensient Technologies.*

In 1887, the name of Meadow Springs was changed to National Distillery under the presidency of August Grau, who expanded its yeast operations under the name of Red Star. By the diversification into yeast, National was able to weather a slump in whiskey prices in 1888. Milwaukee's disastrous Third Ward fire of 1892 destroyed National Distillery's offices on Erie Street. Undaunted, the firm rebuilt. Seeking expansion in 1898, National invested in the Illinois Vinegar Manufacturing Company and the next year purchased a vinegar works started by the Pabst Brewing Company. After a time, however, the Milwaukeeans sold the Illinois firm to Julius Fleischmann of Cincinnati, who went on to develop Fleischmann Yeast. That firm evolved into Standard Brands.

By now, National was ensconced at 79–83 Buffalo Street, where its logo can still be seen above the front entrance. The company's free wet bar made it a popular stop for the beat cops, delivery men and customers visiting the distillery's warehouse to pick cases or wagonloads of National's many labels. Among the brands were Cavalier and Coronation whiskeys; along with Gold Bullion, Livingston, Mistletoe, National, Posthoorn, Roland and Ruby gins.

Many of National's liquor products were especially popular in Milwaukee's so-called "barrel houses," typified by Charles Lubenow's tavern at Twelfth and Walnut Streets and with others serving the hundreds of workers along the Commission Row produce market. At Lubenow's, some thirty barrels of various liquors were always lined up on the sidewalk in front of the place, where drinks on tap went for twenty cents a pint. Many of Lubenow's customers were immigrant Bohemian tailors arriving at 4:00 a.m. and staying on until 7:30 a.m., when they had to report for work. The drinkers received a granite cup of gin and a glass and moved to the gaming tables in the rear room or went bowling in the back third of the building. National's beverages were served in the "best" clubs, as well as in the barrelhouses and taverns. The swell set gathered for after-work drinks at the Milwaukee Club on the corner or gathered at the Country Club on Whitefish Bay Road, the Gentlemen's Driving Club or the Milwaukee Athletic Club.[10]

The less stylish crowd headed to the bars on Jones Island, a narrow strip of land just off Milwaukee's South Side shoreline inhabited by about two thousand Kashubian fishermen and their families. Originally from the Baltic Sea region of Poland, the residents squatted on the mile-long, three-block-wide spit in defiance of the Illinois Steel Company, which said it owned the land. The fishermen were a law unto themselves. As such, things were often wild out on weekends, with no local police presence to keep watch on the eleven taverns there. Some were mere shanties built precariously on stilts

Barrelhouses were popular in Milwaukee until 1917. Here, whiskey is being siphoned into barrels to take to the saloons served by Meadow Springs and National Distilleries. *Photo courtesy of Sensient Technologies.*

over the water. Mainlanders rowed over to visit "Governor" Anton Kanski's saloon or dropped in to see "Admiral" Charles Plambeck, who claimed he had the longest mustache of any bar owner on the island. One visitor said of the Jones Islanders, "All they do in the summer is fish, drink and fight. And in the winter, they don't fish."[11]

By 1916, National and S.C. Herbst were the largest of the Milwaukee distilleries. Herbst had three subsidiaries operating out of the same offices: Benson Creek Distillery, Old Judge Distilling Company and the Old John E. Fitzgeralds Distillery.[12] Herbst was always first and foremost a whiskey man, with his first ad in the *Wine and Spirits Bulletin* appearing in 1904. By then, Herbst was selling his Old Fitzgeralds bourbon in Italy, Germany, France and England, with offices in Chicago, New York, London, Paris, Berlin and Genoa. In 1913, a Herbst ad declared that his Old Fitzgeralds and Old Judge were the last "Old Fashioned Copper Pot Distilled Whiskeys" being made in the United States.[13]

The death warrant for Milwaukee's distilleries came at the onset of Prohibition. The last ten gallons of National's whiskey were hauled off by company trucker Wallace Ward, who stored his cache behind his furnace and waited just a bit too long before sampling the goods. By the time he got around to it, most had evaporated, and only about one-third remained.

In 1919, realizing that the temperance movement had gained the upper hand, National's management voted to change the company name to Red Star Yeast & Products Company, effectively getting out of the booze business for the time being. When Prohibition was repealed, the firm cranked up its stills and began producing gin once again, along with beer. By November 1933, the entire fifth floor of its Third Ward warehouse was packed with hundreds of thirty-gallon crocks loaded with fermenting sloe gin berries merrily bubbling away.

In addition, between 1933 and 1936, Red Star was involved in a court battle over the use of the National Distilling name. National Distillers Products Corporation of New York claimed that since Red Star was no longer using that title, it had a right to acquire it. In 1938, Red Star finally agreed to give up all rights to the National corporate tagline. At only $20,800, the sale price was a steal. Red Star then turned its attention to yeast and vinegar as main products and changed its name again in 1962 to Universal Foods Corporation. In 2000, Universal Foods became Sensient Technologies Corporation, which sold its Red Star Yeast & Products division in 2001 to the French-based Lesaffre et Compagnie, ending an interesting chapter in the city's distilling history.[14]

Great Lakes Distillery

It took several generations before spirits were distilled again in Milwaukee. As the first state distiller since Prohibition, Great Lakes Distillery started producing in a converted dairy plant and then moved to Milwaukee's Walker's Point for additional space. Owned by Guy Rehorst, the distillery turns out premium vodka, gin and other refreshing beverages, bragging that its handcrafted spirits are "made one drop at a time."

Before opening his firm, Rehorst was a home-brewer/winemaker and naturally became curious about distilling. He wondered why a patron could walk into a bar or restaurant and get any number of locally made craft beers but couldn't find any craft spirits. Since Rehorst noted that all the spirits seemed to come from overseas or from a small handful of distilleries in Kentucky, he started doing research and became hooked. The more he learned, the more he wanted to open his own facility. The fact that he discovered that Milwaukee and Wisconsin had a great distilling tradition and that Prohibition had killed the local industry made him want to try his hand at the process all the more.

Rehorst's grandfather, Alex Rehorst, was a Milwaukee cop during Prohibition, a law not really supported or enforced by most of the local police. There are stories of his grandfather getting invited into speakeasies on his beat for a little something to warm him up on a cold night. The family folktale, of course, was that he never shut down one of these places on his beat. Rehorst's great-grandfather, Marcel Ciepluch, opened a tavern/store

Great Lakes Distillery brands. *Photo courtesy of Great Lakes Distillery.*

sin 1909 on Ninth and Arthur Streets, which he operated before, during and after Prohibition.

To raise funds, Rehorst sold Great Lakes Media, a high-tech manufacturer of compact discs, which he had launched earlier, and headed to his bank to ask for more financial help. Initially, the dubious financiers had a good laugh about his idea. Yet since his first venture already had a strong repayment track record, they eventually took his vision for Great Lakes Distillery seriously and helped him out with a loan.

There weren't a lot of educational opportunities in distilling when Rehorst started thinking about opening his plant. He contacted an equipment manufacturer, one that offered a distilling class, and also took a short course at Michigan State University. In between these learning opportunities, Rehorst also studied the distilling process at several other small distilleries. The recipe for his first vodka product was developed over a long time, with Rehorst testing grain varieties, trying different yeast and experimenting with filtering media and times. For his venture, he was joined by master distiller Doug MacKenzie, a former world-class speed skater who loved the creativity of making spirits, and sales manager Ryan Rappis, departing the world of medical sales for the "glamor" of the liquor industry.

The new firm's first location was in Milwaukee's Riverwest neighborhood, with Rehorst signing the lease in January 2005. The firm was finally able to sell a tested and completed product in October 2006. When the first batch of Rehorst Premium Milwaukee Vodka was poured and sipped, everyone on the team was elated, especially after surviving all those years of research and wading through tons of licensing red tape.

That initial space seemed huge until the first container of bottles arrived from France. Then, two years into production, Great Lakes needed more room but couldn't make it work in the existing building. So the company moved to Walkers Point on the city's near South Side, utilizing ninety-five hundred square feet of space in a venerable former warehouse. Because Great Lakes was also increasing its production, Rehorst needed to secure a hazardous occupancy permit, which required special sprinkler and ventilation considerations. While the governmental application process to open a distillery could be intimidating, federal employees and local officials were always helpful as the distillery blossomed. Once they understood that Rehorst was opening a small craft distillery and not a large ethanol plant, they better understood the company's needs.

The firm's first invoice went to the now-closed Long Necks Brewpub in Big Bend. The bar manager from there, Jason Neu, now works in the Great

Left: Guy Rehorst (left), Ryan Rappis (center) and Doug MacKenzie (right) of Great Lake Distillery produce exceptionally smooth vodka, gin and other spirits on Milwaukee's near South Side. *Photo courtesy of Great Lakes Distillery.*

Below: Great Lakes Distillery interior. *Photo courtesy of Great Lakes Distillery.*

Tour groups love the experience of checking out the inner workings of Great Lakes Distillery. There is plenty of opportunity to explore and ask questions of the guides. *Photo courtesy of Great Lakes Distillery.*

Lakes tasting room and helps area bars develop their new signature drinks. As the workforce expanded, it wasn't long before a dozen additional accounts were secured with taverns, restaurants and several major liquor stores in the Greater Milwaukee area. Concentrating on Southeast Wisconsin for its first four years, Great Lakes began pushing into northern Illinois, Nebraska, Minnesota and Tennessee, realizing that it was a lot easier to get into a market than it was to garner support and retain staying power. Facing the same hurdles as many boutique distillers, Great Lakes quickly learned that distributors tended to give the most attention to the big brands, those that were easier to sell.

However, Rehorst and his group pushed ahead despite other challenges, such as high excise taxes, with the company paying about four times what a brewery owed for producing the same amount of alcohol. Just to pour samples in the tasting room, Great Lakes also needed to have several laws changed at the state level. Rehorst finally found Democratic representative Pedro Colon, who was willing to help him with the appropriate legislation. Subsequently, the company can now dispense samples and sell cocktails and bottles from the distillery. In late 2010, the distillery also received permission from the federal government to begin a bottle reuse program.

By volume, vodka is the most popular spirit in the United States, and not surprisingly, that variety of drink is Great Lakes bestseller, with rum and

Above: A wide range of gift items is available in the Great Lakes Distillery gift shop, always appropriate for remembering a tour of the company's Milwaukee plant. *Photo courtesy of Great Lakes Distillery.*

Below: Great Lakes Distillery fans belly up to the bar during hosted special events, tastings and related happenings. They can certainly be guaranteed of a good pour. *Photo courtesy of Great Lakes Distillery.*

gin gaining more attention from appreciative fans. The firm's vodka was followed by a gin in 2007, a smooth liquor that captured a Double Gold at the 2008 San Francisco World Spirits Competition.[15] Great Lakes' citrus and honey flavored vodka then snared a World Spirits gold medal in 2009. Proud of their offerings, Rehorst and his crew love winning awards, and there are usually a few toasts to celebrate when the medals are presented. Yet even better than such industry awards are the e-mail or Facebook compliments.

The distillery keeps expanding its brand offerings. A line of Artisan Series brandies are displayed in 375-mililiter bottles with labels painted by distiller MacKenzie's mother, artist Claire MacKenzie. Great Lakes also makes grappa, kirschwasser, Pear Brandy Eau-de-Vie, Amerique 1912 Absinthe Verte and Amerique 1912 Absinthe Rouge.[16]

Great Lakes Distillery Absinthe. *Photo courtesy of Great Lakes Distillery.*

Above: From experience, Great Lakes Distillery can easily adjust its output because the manufacturer carefully keeps track of inventory and knows which of its spirits sell best during the appropriate season. *Photo courtesy of Great Lakes Distillery.*

Left: Workers at Great Lakes Distillery use only top-quality ingredients in the making of their spirits. *Photo courtesy of Great Lakes Distillery.*

Because everything is done in small batches, Great Lakes can easily adjust its output. The management watches the distributors' inventory, and when sales of vodka spike in late spring, the plant has already anticipated the growing demand and increased volume in time for the rush. For Rehorst, most of the fun comes in making what he likes and then seeing a drinker sample a Great Lakes beverage for the first time, noting that he or she loves it.

Launched in 2010 with a large "coming-out" gala at the distillery, Great Lakes' Roaring Dan's Rum is produced from fermented Grade A sugar cane molasses. Before a second distillation, pure Wisconsin maple syrup is added. The rum is then aged in a combination of new charred American white oak barrels and used bourbon barrels. The liquor's name is attributed to Dan Seavey, the only man ever arrested for piracy on the Great Lakes. Seavey owned a saloon and brothel in Milwaukee, leaving his hometown to join the Alaskan gold rush. Arriving back in Milwaukee without having struck it rich, Seavey still had enough stash to purchase the schooner *Wanderer*, a hardy vessel that he used to haul lumber and grain. On the side, he smuggled poached venison and prostitutes between Great Lakes ports. Supposedly, more than a few of these "soiled doves" even festively plied their trade aboard the *Wanderer* when docked.

On June 11, 1908, Seavey hijacked the schooner *Nellie Johnson* in Frankfort, Michigan, after getting the captain and crew drunk on good Milwaukee-made whiskey and enthusiastically tossing those unfortunates overboard. Luckily, nobody drowned, and the men were able to swim to shore. As they were splashing their way to safety, shocked to sensibility by the cold lake surf, Seavey hurriedly pulled anchor and piloted the captured boat to Chicago. There, he sold its cargo of highly valued cedar posts to lumber dealers noted for not asking too many questions. Seavey then took the *Nellie Johnson* back across the lake to Michigan, where he had secretly docked the *Wanderer* in a small bay. By this time, federal authorities had heard of the incident, became alarmed and ordered the *Tuscarora*, a government revenue cutter based in Milwaukee, to pursue Seavey.

But the Milwaukeean was already back aboard his original vessel and again roaming Lake Michigan's open water. The gunboat, under the command of Captain

Roaring Dan's Rum. *Photo courtesy of Great Lakes Distillery.*

The *Tuscarora*, a federal revenue cutter, pursued alleged pirate Dan Seavey around Lake Michigan, capturing the miscreant after firing a warning shot. *Photo courtesy of Great Lakes Distillery.*

Preston Ueberroth, carried an experienced deputy federal marshal by the name of Thomas H. Currier out of Chicago. On June 29, after an extended fox hunt across the lake, Ueberroth finally caught up with the *Wanderer*, and marshal Currier ordered a warning shot fired from the *Tuscarora*'s forward gun. With the *Wanderer* finally stopped, Ueberroth sent a well-armed marine boarding party to seize the forty-three-year-old renegade captain.[17]

Initially being taken to Chicago to face the piracy accusation, Seavey instead was charged with the "unauthorized removal of a vessel on which he had once been a seaman." The lesser charge was ordered because several years earlier, Seavey had actually been a deckhand aboard the *Nellie Johnson*. The redoubtable defendant was released on bond because he maintained that he had won the good *Nellie* in a poker game and its owner did not show up in court to dispute his claim. Seavey returned to the shipping trade, albeit more legally. For all that Great Lakes cavorting in his younger days, Seavey passed away in a nursing home in Peshtigo, Wisconsin, on Valentine's Day 1949 at age eighty-four. He died "a lonely man," wrote one journalist at the time.[18]

Since Great Lakes' launch, other Wisconsin distilleries have also opened. Yahara Bay Distillers in Madison, Death's Head in Door County and 45th Parallel Vodka in New Richmond have each carved out niches that admirably serve their legions of fiercely devoted followers.

There's a Tavern in the Town

Lager beer of Best and Company
2 glasses for 5 cents!
Morning lunch
Evenings we invite you to enjoy humorous
entertainment with piano accompaniment.
—Advertisement for A.C. Kuhn tavern in the Banner und Volksfreund
(translated from the German), August 18, 1859

One can't talk about Milwaukee's beer and distilling history without discussing its noteworthy bar and tavern scene, which is first noted in 1837, when Louis Trayser opened his Zum Deutschen Little Tavern at State and Water Streets.[1]

As early as 1843, pioneer historian James Buck recorded 138 taverns in Milwaukee, an average of 1 per forty residents. Most were "rum holes," rather like neighborhood taverns but less reputable. These dives got their name from cheap rum, which was liberally dispensed, and from their being dug back into the hillside along the Milwaukee River. The places were usually boarded up in front and had crude bars, over which was served low-grade home-brews and challet. This latter drink was a fearsome concoction of fermented wild berries, watercress, rum and limestone. The first German settlers around Milwaukee developed potent *essig whiskey heimer*, which first showed up early in 1839. Since no beer was initially available, farmers mixed whiskey and vinegar with a dash of ever-present limestone thrown in to put a "head" on it for added value. Many of the rum holes had back rooms, often dank tunnels, where the owner could store his stock. Some of these passages were jumbled with cots and straw ticks where men, women and children could lodge temporarily. Up to three hundred immigrants were arriving daily in Milwaukee and needed shelter; they usually headed to the closest place they could find near the docks. These "taverns" acted as social centers, banks offering short-term credit, travelers' aid societies, forums and even as lovers' rendezvous.[2]

At the start of the Civil War, historians estimated that there was 1 bar for each ninety-eight Milwaukee residents.[3] The list of saloons in the city covered nearly three pages of the city directory in 1873, numbering 502 establishments. Newspaper reports related the economic importance of the beverage industry throughout this era. According to one account:

> *Allowing a fair average of $300 as the cost of each of these saloons, it will be seen that over $150,000 are invested in this business. These places employ about two thousand persons including the beer peddlers of our breweries, and at a fair average of three quarter-barrels a day, nearly four hundred barrels of beer are daily dealt out by the glass and by the measure. At ten dollars a barrel, the brewers receive a daily return of about $4,000 or about $28,000 a week. At a profit of three dollars a Quarter, about $3,000 are daily swept into the coffers of the keepers. As the profits on liquors equal that of beer, the sum of $10,000 is daily distributed in the way of profits by the bibulous portion of our community. In these estimates we have not included bottled beer and white-beer trade of the city.*[4]

In the late 1800s Milwaukee, a drinker seeking a good thirst-quenching could select from at least thirty-five hundred drinking establishments ranging from the aforementioned dilapidated rum holes to fancy bars in highbrow hotels. About three hundred were owned and managed by women, most of them widows who had inherited the places from their deceased husbands.[5] The plethora of bars extended well into the 1940s and 1950s and allegedly made it easier for Milwaukee native son and noted actor Spencer Tracy to occasionally—and only briefly—escape the long arm of his paramour, actress Katharine Hepburn, and the hounding of his press agents. It was said that Tracy often returned to the city, sometimes hanging out with fellow Milwaukeean and acting buddy Pat O'Brien. The two would "go to ground" at least for a couple of days of convivial conversation and genial cavorting before resurfacing as if nothing had happened.[6]

While most people enjoyed their beverages in a responsible manner, others needed some assistance with what could grow into a drinking challenge. There were several facilities where those in need could retire for drying out. In 1893, health services were added to the ministry of the School Sisters of St. Francis, with the opening of their Sacred Heart Sanitarium adjacent to the motherhouse on South Layton Avenue. The well-appointed sanitarium was the first of its kind in Milwaukee and became well known throughout the United States and Europe for its treatment of "mental and nervous disorders," often a euphemism for alcoholism. No names were listed in the sanitarium's record books, with "clients" noted only by a number tacked on the doors to the rooms.[7]

In 2010, the number of Milwaukee-area bars, taverns and other outlets selling alcohol was still impressive. With eighteen liquor-selling establishments, sixteen of which that sold beer and liquor and two that sold only beer, the Milwaukee suburb of Franklin had percentage-wise one alcohol-selling retailer for every 1,872 residents. However, twelve of these outlets were not taverns but gas stations, convenience stores or grocers. Despite this variety, it still meant that tiny Franklin had the highest concentration, in terms of population, among Milwaukee County's nineteen municipalities. Wauwatosa was tied with Shorewood for second, followed by Hales Corners and then Milwaukee. Brown Deer had only one alcohol retailer for every 5,860 residents. River Hills had none at all. Milwaukee proper had 294 licensees for its 580,000 residents.[8]

The Scheneck and Schwindt saloon was one of the fanciest places in early downtown, a prime site eventually occupied by Gimbel's Department Store. Visiting Gimbel's years later, old-timers could still point out where the S&S bar used to overlook the river, where patrons watched the water traffic as they drank their beer. Later, Henry Wehr owned the saloon. Across the street was the upscale Browning and King's haberdashery, in case a drinker needed a change of shirt collars. Of course, there were places more lowbrow, such as John Fogg's Cannibal's Rendezvous on Jones Island, where the Kashubian Polish fishermen gathered for their nickel drafts poured from barrels tagged as "wooden bladders."

True to their heritage, the newly arrived Germans were also responsible for the *biergarten*, giant brewery parks that served gallons of beer amid potted palms and other expansive floral arrangements situated among the tables. Flotillas of waiters in starched white aprons sailed through the crowds, trays laden with steins carried by one hand high over their heads. In the days before child labor laws, the bucket boy, or *kesseljunge*, was given the job of rushing back and forth from the factory floor to the closest tavern. Others carried smaller takeout jugs nicknamed "growlers," which are still popular at many Milwaukee brewpubs. Yet there were occasional limits. At the W. Toepfer & Sons Ironworks, beer drinking was limited to between 9:30 a.m. and 3:00 p.m. The Germans also loved picnics, concerts and *Saengerfests*, those family-oriented social events at which beer drinking and *Gemuetlichkeit*, or good feeling and fellowship, were linked.[9]

Terrace Gardens, a "public pleasure garden" and a popular venue for outdoor concerts and picnics by the community's beer-imbibing Germans was landscaped on the site of pioneer settler Frank Lackner's former home. However, in 1868, John Pritzlaff, a wealthy member of Trinity Lutheran Church who operated a wholesale hardware business, gave his congregation that large lot at the corner of North Ninth Street and West Highland Avenue, and the gardens closed. Yet despite the continued growth in the congregation, it took another ten years for construction to begin on the present church. When the cornerstone for the church was laid on July 8, 1878, an estimated one thousand people attended the ceremony. Trinity was designated a Milwaukee historical landmark in 1967.[10]

One of the most popular beer gardens was Quentin's Park on Walnut Street, where locals held picnics and sipped refreshing beverages atop what was reportedly a Native American burial mound. Schlitz purchased the property and erected a fancy pavilion, with bubbling fountains illuminated with one hundred gas lamps, four white flagpoles at the entrance and full-throated opera singers for entertainment.

H. Kemper's beer garden was built in 1850 in Milwaukee's burgeoning main street business neighborhood. A short time later, the affable Pius Dreher built his beer palace beneath a stand of stately trees on the block bordered by State, Fourteenth and Fifteenth Streets and Prairie Avenue. The gardens sported five hundred tables able to seat three thousand persons. Another famous site was Ludwig's on the River, at the Pleasant Street Bridge, where "in a setting of greenery and shade," wine, ale and lager was served amid "a display of exotic and redolent plants." Typical of the men who operated these facilities was Otto Osthoff, manager and lessee of an expansive outdoor playground called Schlitz Park. Osthoff was born at Bielefield, a village near Berlin, and served seven years in the Prussian army. In 1864, he came to America, landing in New York, where he remained for a year and a half. Osthoff meandered on to Rochester, New York, where he managed a hotel. In 1867, he came to Milwaukee and rented a small brewery, which he operated for three years. He then became manager and

The Whitefish Bay Resort, north of downtown Milwaukee, was a typical outdoors beer garden in the early twentieth century. Captain Fredrick Pabst opened the facility in 1889, attracting upwards of fifteen thousand people on warm Sunday afternoons. The resort presented concerts, offered Ferris wheel rides and plenty of beer. Visitors came via foot or bicycle, steam train or aboard the *Bloomer Girl*, an excursion boat carrying passengers from a downtown dock to the resort. *Photos courtesy of the Historic Pabst Mansion.*

lessee of a Schlitz facility at Seventh and Walnut in May 1880. He and his partner, Jacob Litt, began presenting musicals and light opera there under the name Bijou Theater Company in 1893.[11]

Osthoff and his wife, Paulina Bittmann Osthoff, then built a hotel in Elkhart Lake, Wisconsin, in 1886. Originally called Hotel Münsterland, the name was later changed to the Osthoff Hotel. During the Prohibition era, it operated as a gaming casino and featured a well-known speakeasy drawing the uppercrust crowd from around southeastern Wisconsin. On a darker side, it was also allegedly a haunt favored by Milwaukee's 1930s-era gangsters. Over the next generations, the property underwent a number of renovations, with the AAA Four Diamond Osthoff Resort and adjoining condos opening in 1989. The current facility maintains a Germanic theme, featuring the casual Otto's Restaurant, along with higher-end dining.[12]

One of the most famous beer gardens, the richly ornamented Schlitz Palm Garden and Hotel, opened on July 3, 1896. An extravagant celebration staged on July 6 and 7 featured concert works by Offenbach,

Zeller and similar notable composers. Designed by architects Kirchen & Rose, the skylighted space was replete with artificial ponds and plenty of gurgling fountains amid the abundance of flora.[13] For the next quarter of a century, under the management of August Pleiss and Philip Heck, the garden attracted all ages and social strata of clientele who came to listen to Jos. Clauder's Orchestra on the bandstand and to sip a brewski. Often, boatloads of tourists from Chicago took excursion boats for the day to visit Milwaukee and tour the Palm Garden. The pleasure palace was also the site of major conventions, such as those staged by the International Association of Fire Chiefs in 1911 and the Ancient and Honorable Artillery of Boston, plus sports banquets and other civic affairs that the Schlitz Brewery was happy to sponsor.

Knowing where to find Milwaukee voters, New Jersey governor Woodrow Wilson made one of his first campaign appearances at the Palm Garden in his bid for the Democratic presidential nomination in the 1912 White House race. Between three speeches he gave in Milwaukee on Sunday, March 24, just before he set out for a Pabst Theater appearance, Wilson asked to see the Palm Garden, the city's most noted tourist attraction. He mingled with the happy crowd, but "the distinguished visitor did not try the brew," according to newspaper reports. Perhaps that visit among Milwaukee's dedicated beer drinkers and political activities helped Wilson secure his party's nod at its August convention.[14]

Among Wilson's opponents was the Progressive candidate Teddy Roosevelt, who, incidentally, was shot later that year in Milwaukee. On October 14, 1912, Bavarian-born John Schrank, a New York tavern keeper, wounded the Bull Mooser, who shrugged off the incident and launched into an extended speech. Also running against Wilson in that election was Socialist candidate Eugene Victor Debs, whose vice-presidential running mate Emil Seidel was a reformist mayor of Milwaukee from 1910 to 1912. Seidel, the first Socialist mayor of a major city in the United States, had just lost his bid for a second two-year term to Gerhard Adolph Bading, the son of a Lutheran pastor and a fusion candidate favored by Milwaukee's joined-at-the-wallet Republican and Democratic business establishment.[15]

An able politician, first elected alderman in 1908, Seidel knew his constituents and their needs, often meeting with them in the city's taverns and beer gardens. While the power structure didn't care much for Seidel and his politics, the average Joe Beer Drinker thought the bespectacled, earnest former patternmaker was tops. He was considered one of them, although Seidel was a reformist who shut down Milwaukee's brothels and gin mills along a wild stretch of the dockside Water Street. Locals loved him because

Seidel's accomplishments included introducing the country's first workers' compensation program in 1911, adult and worker education classes, free medical and dental examinations for schoolchildren and the first fire and police commission. So it seemed natural to honor the mayor in the best way possible. "Seidel" became the nickname for a beer mug, which in the minds of Milwaukeeans makes a much better memorial than a mere statue.[16]

After the Palm Garden was closed, the hall was renovated into the Garden Theater, showcasing silent movies and early talkies. It went through other morphings before being demolished in 1963. The Shops of Grand Avenue mall opened in 1982 on the site.

Enterprising Milwaukee brewers such as Frederick Pabst, always eager to expand his markets and show the world how to really drink beer, carried this garden concept elsewhere. In the 1890s, he traveled to Manhattan and set up a beer garden in Times Square, at "the Circle" at 58th Street and at "the Harlem" at 125th Street. He even imported a clutch of Milwaukee serving staff to show the New Yorkers "how to do it."[17]

The city's taverns and biergartens doubled as the era's social centers, where Herr Schultz and Herr Schmidt could relax over their steins and rounds of card playing. While cribbage, euchre and poker were popular, sheepshead, or "sheephead," was *the* game of choice, particularly among the Germans. This is a trick-taking card game related to the skat family, an Americanized version of a game that originated in Central Europe in the late eighteenth century under the German name *Schafkopf*. Although Schafkopf literally means "sheepshead," the term may have been derived from Middle High German and referred to playing cards on an overturned barrel (from *kopfen*, meaning "playing cards," and *schaff*, meaning "a barrel"—usually a beer barrel).[18] At any rate, it was the perfect tavern game for fun-loving Milwaukeeans.

The city was dotted with these grand getaways, some more imposing than others, but each with its fan base. In the Menomonee River near the Melms Brewery "was a verdant spot ideally fit for the pouring fourth of the golden drink," which eventually was replaced by a house. Some tavern structures had more ignominious ends once they outlived their usefulness. *The Pioneer History of Milwaukee* relates that "Belden's Old Home Saloon, now No. 1 Spring Street, was removed this year [1896], July 14, to make room for the present block. It was placed upon a scow, carried to the South Side, and placed upon the west side of Reed street, near where the Union Depot now stands, where it was subsequently burned."[19]

Milwaukee is still proud of its German bars and eateries, although they are becoming fewer and fewer, with the loss of such stalwarts as John Ernest

Café, which opened in 1878 on East Ogden Avenue and closed in 2001. Another, Zur Krone, left its Walker's Point Home in that same year, finding a new home in Thiensville, Wisconsin, where it eventually shuttered for good after several years. The cozy, original place, with its large round *stammtisch* in the corner window, was taken over by the Crazy Water restaurant.[20]

Mader's may still be one of the country's most notable German restaurants, opened in 1902 by Charles Mader and still operating in 2011. Originally called the Comfort, Mader boasted of his "soft" wooden chairs and oaken tables. Dinner, including tip and beverage, was twenty cents, and steins of Cream City beer were three cents each, two for a nickel. If a patron spent five cents on beer, his lunch was free. Originally on Plankinton Avenue, Mader moved his restaurant to North Third Street (now Old World Third Street). With Prohibition looming, Mader hung a sign in his window, proclaiming: "Prohibition is near at hand. Prepare for the worst. Stock up now! Today and tomorrow there's beer. Soon there'll be only the lake."

When Prohibition's screws began turning in 1919, Mader turned his attention to a big kitchen that became famous for the sauerbraten, wiener schnitzel and pork shank dished out in heaping servings. Since Milwaukeeans were never ones to forego a meal, even one sans beer, Mader's did happily make it to that jubilant, cheering night of April 7, 1933, when its legion of barmen poured the first legal steins in the city. The end of Prohibition was announced at midnight from the restaurant's commodious barroom via the city's only radio station. When Charles Mader died in 1938, his sons, Gus and George, took over. Gus's son, Victor, joined his father in running the restaurant in 1964, with the young Mader taking control when his father died in 1982. The Knight's Bar at Mader's remains reminiscent of an old-fashioned *bierstubbe*.[21]

Ratzsch's Restaurant was launched in 1904, when Chef Otto Hermann opened his Hermann's Café in downtown Milwaukee. A few years later, his stepdaughter, Helen, came from Germany to live and work in the café. Prior to World War I, Karl August Ratzsch Sr. was a young man touring the United States. Due to the outbreak of war, he stayed in the States, settling in Milwaukee, and began working with Helen. After a ten-year courtship, the couple married. They purchased the café and relocated it to the current location in the prestigious Colby-Abbot Building, built in 1883 on Milwaukee Street. The couple then changed the name to Karl Ratzsch's. Karl (Papa) and Helen continued operation of the restaurant until 1962, when Karl Jr. became owner. His son, Josef, bought out Karl in the mid-1990s and sold the property to a new management team in 2003.[22]

To help keep their heritages alive, several of Milwaukee's German cultural organizations built their own clubhouses, now open to the public. In 1934, several Bavarian societies leased the property between the Milwaukee River and Port Washington Road south of West Silver Spring Drive. By 1943, the club had built several high-quality soccer fields and a huge dining room with a large bar offering German and local beers. The original clubhouse is now the site of the La Quinta Suites. The property was sold in 1967, when the United German Societies built the Bavarian Inn at 700 Lexington Boulevard. The club's fifteen-acre Old Heidelberg Park, with its stages and gazebo, hosts festivals, dances, picnics and other events in the true tradition of Milwaukee's German community.[23]

The Donauschwaben Vergnügungsverein and three other Donauschwaben clubs—the Apatiner Verein, the Mucsi Familienverein and the Milwaukee Sport Club—opened a complex in the mid-1960s. Serving a population of Germans whose ancestors once lived along the Danube River in the old Kingdom of Hungary, the complex in Menomonee Falls has a restaurant, halls to rent, a picnic area and soccer fields. It is much like the traditional beer gardens of previous generations.[24]

Several other German taverns and beer halls survived the years, including the venerable Kegel's Inn, established in 1924. Now managed by Rob and Jim Kegel, the building still has its original leaded glass and heavy wooden beams.[25] Paul Elhlert managed several bars on the East Side, one of which was a tavern at 1216 East Brady Street, now housing the Up and Under Pub, one of the city's premier blues clubs.[26] Nodde's Bar at the corner of Warren Avenue and Brady Street was another local hangout in the 1950s and is now called the Nomad World Pub, the first of several bars owned by tavern/eatery entrepreneur Mike Eitel of the Diablos Rojos Restaurant Group.[27]

If one knows what to look for, numerous "tied house" taverns are still readily seen around Milwaukee. These were bars owned or operated by the breweries, selling only that particular brand. Some of these remaining buildings were mapped and annotated by the dedicated supporters of Milwaukee's Museum of Beer and Brewing, a group eyeing part of the old Pabst brewing complex for its eventual home. Most of the structures the group has identified still have brewery company emblems over the doors, on the outside walls or on the roofs.[28]

Schlitz, Best (later known as Pabst) and Blatz brewing companies purchased some two hundred corner lots in 1884 alone. An article in the *Milwaukee Sentinel* stated that the fact "that there should be room for a saloon for every 130 inhabitants (including men, women and children) has given the city the name of being the saloonkeeper's paradise." The article continued, saying that it

> is hardly possible, however, that all of these saloons could be profitably continued were it not for the backing of the brewers. The brewers have invested an enormous aggregate of capital in the business of brewing beer, and have a vital interest in having the demand for beer kept up. Within the past two years, the export trade has been affected by a more active competition, and in order to utilize the full strength of their productive facilities, local brewers have seen the need of maintaining the home trade.[29]
>
> Rather than merely supplying stock and fixtures to saloonkeepers who might otherwise prove untrustworthy or unbusinesslike, the breweries took it upon themselves to erect their own tavern buildings with the result that "[I]t secures the erection of better buildings in place of the wretched structures occupied by the proprietors of low groceries, and better order will be maintained."

All this development was viewed with skepticism by the paper, which commented that saloon sites were being acquired even in the better residential portions of the city and "every property owner knows that they do not enhance the value of his adjoining property, and although he may be a good patron of the saloon, he does not care to have it for his next door neighbor."[30]

Early in his career at Schlitz, company president Joseph Uihlein led the drive to purchase such strategic corner locations around town. Uihlein realized he needed to secure these sites for building saloons to sell the Schlitz brand. This aggressive push thus edged out his competitors, who were also eagerly seeking to entrench themselves in the market. Schlitz's prime real estate holdings proved to be valuable when the brewery was forced to suspend beer production during Prohibition. When the cash-strapped company needed a financial kick during the ensuing Depression, many of its locations were subsequently sold to oil companies for their gas stations. Despite losing these valuable properties, it was a necessary procedure. The money garnered from the real estate transactions helped keep Schlitz afloat in the financially grim 1930s.[31]

Several of the Schlitz locales remain bars or have morphed into restaurants. The Little Schlitz Pub at 2501 West Greenfield Avenue, later became Benjamin Briggs Pub. A blue and white ceramic Schlitz mosaic still adorns the outside wall near the front door, and there's a faded ghost sign—"Drink Schlitz"—on the west wall of the building.[32] Among the early proprietors who ran the tavern were Henry Raasch (1905–06); Joseph Zdroyk (1907–08); Louis Mikulecky (1909); Joseph and Helen Zdroyk, later a widow (1910–11); and William Schaefer (1912–20). The 1920 city directory indicated that the place had become a soft drink parlor, mostly likely because of Prohibition's regulations.

In 1922, the building, sans its bar or saloon fixtures, was sold to Frank and Mary Patock, who continued to run it as a soda fountain. After her husband's death in 1924 and with the repeal of the Eighteenth Amendment, Mrs. Patock obtained a permit to operate the facility as a tavern and remodeled it in the style of an English inn. In the late 1940s, the building went through a succession of owners, including Walter and Rose Orlowski and George and Phyllis Schauer. The building, designated a Milwaukee Historic Site, was purchased in 2009 by Raul Varela Rodriquez and renamed Club Fiesta. All managers and owners over the years demonstrate the changing ethnic demographics of its South Side neighborhood.[33]

In the late 1990s, Dave Sobelman and his wife, Melanie, restored a marvelous old Schlitz tavern at 1900 West St. Paul Avenue, deep in the industrial Menomonee Valley. Factory workers mingle with faculty and students from nearby Marquette University, office personnel, truckers and others from all walks of life flocking to Sobelman's for its giant hamburgers. A large Schlitz globe logo can be seen on the third-floor façade.

The Three Brothers Serbian Restaurant at 2414 South St. Clair Avenue in Bay View also sports a giant Schlitz globe atop its cupola entrance, hence its original name: the Globe Tavern. The hospitable restaurant's low-key charm, augmented by made-from-scratch burek, musaka and kashkaval, has earned raves from *Gourmet* magazine, *Bon Vivant* and other foodie publications. The father of current proprietor Branko Radiecevich purchased it in 1950, shortly after the family emigrated from war-torn Yugoslavia.

A former Schlitz tied house can still be found at Holton and Clarke at the north end of the Holton Street Bridge, at 2414 South St. Clair in Bay View. A giant Schlitz Globe is perched on its rooftop. Schlitz built another Mike Eitel property, the Trocadero at 1758 North Water Street, for barkeep Frank Druml in 1890 for $8,000. The building was also a rooming house for newly arrived immigrants who worked in the tanneries across Water Street. The Main Event, a now-shuttered blues and jazz club at 3418 North Martin Luther King Drive, was also once a tied house.

Club Garibaldi at 2501 South Superior Street is just across the Hoan Bridge spanning Milwaukee's harbor in Bay View. In 1908, the building opened as

A Spirited History of Milwaukee Brews and Booze

a tavern whose then-owner eventually moved farther down Russell Avenue. He opened another bar in the neighborhood made up predominately of Piedemontese Italians. The Schlitz Brewery eventually took over, adding the expansive wood bar still seen today. A back hall was added in 1927, and the Giuseppe Garibaldi Society, a fraternal order formed by northern Italian immigrants, began meeting there. The society purchased the building about 1941, leasing the tavern operation to Tag Grotelueschen and Joe Dean, two former East Side bartenders at the Points East Pub on Lyon Street.[31]

Among the remaining Pabst tied houses is Regano's Roman Coin at 1004 East Brady Street, a well-known East Side landmark at Astor and Brady Streets. Originally topped by an ornate cupola, the structure was built in 1890 by well-known architect Otto Schrank, who also designed the Pabst Theater. The use of such professionals was typical of the breweries, which wanted to ensure the highest-quality look for their properties. Joe Regano purchased this building in 1996, and his daughter, Teri, is the current owner.[35] Restorante Bartolotta at 7616 West State Street in Wauwatosa was also a Pabst tavern, as was Slim McGinn's Irish Pub at 338 First Street. The latter building had formerly been owned by Milwaukee restaurateur Johnny (Johnny V) Vassallo, who operated it as Smugglers. Richard (Slim) McGinn was the former bar manager at the Harp on Juneau before branching out on his own.

A Miller tied house can also be found at the corner of Hubbard and Garfield in the aptly named Brewers Hill district, once home to numerous brewery managers and workers. Nearby is the building once housing the fabled Humboldt Gardens, another Miller tavern at the corner of Humboldt and North Avenue. In another life, it morphed into Zak's nightclub and was unoccupied as of 2010. A windstorm in late 2010 peeled off much of the Cream City brick façade.

Notable Milwaukee Bars

Not long ago, a flatlander from New Lenox, Illinois, visited an in-law on Weil Street in what was once a Polish working-class neighborhood now called the more neutrally encompassing Riverwest. He stood in the middle of the intersection and marveled that there were taverns on each corner and one in the middle of every block as far as he could see. Each establishment had its own fiercely dedicated clientele.

In the early twentieth century, Milwaukee licensed 2,440 taverns, 6,767 bartenders, 2,630 pinball machines, seven horse-drawn junk wagons and fourteen handcarts. Author and Democratic political operative Harold Gauer published a series of books about growing up on Milwaukee's East Side in the 1930s and 1940s, with some of his best tales focusing on the city's taverns. "For some good souls, it was a confessional. For the depressed, it was a pool in which sorrow was drowned, and for boasters, appreciative listeners were always there. The tavern served all the purposes of the classic Greek marketplace, the desert oasis, and the baths of ancient Rome," Gauer rhapsodized.[36]

In the 1930s, taverns were usually in clapboard buildings, unlike the more genteel tied houses of the previous generation—although *schweinbacke* (hog jowls) and bratwurst perfumed both. Among the better-known hideaways were Ernie & Mary's, Frank & Sally's, Sophie's Place, Shorty's Doghouse, Ma's, Joe's, Steve's and others of that ilk. Emil Koeller's roadhouse gardens on Green Bay Road offered plenty of cheek-to-cheek dancing when Belly Snider played the piano and Uncle Nats set forth on the drums. There, the waiters serving beers, Old Farm rye whiskey and sloe gin didn't need any experience. The joke was that if wait staff applicants could walk without falling over their own feet, they got a job.[37]

Dirty Helen's Sunflower Inn on St. Paul Avenue opened in 1926, serving no food but sneaking drinks to its more upscale clientele. During the Depression, "Dirty" Helen Cromwell, a devotee of Old Fitzgerald bourbon, gleefully served abundant amounts of what she exclaimed were "hard drinks for hard times." The Sunflower shuttered in 1959. Peter and Mary Sigan opened Mary's Log Cabin tavern and restaurant shortly after World War I at Clinton Street and Greenfield Avenue. It became a rooming house during Prohibition. Peter died in 1933, and typical of the day, his widow carried on, becoming noted among the factory workers at nearby Allen Bradley plant for her "Deep Fat Fried Chicken Jamboree" served on Saturday nights.[38]

During the late 1930s, up-and-coming young politicos, writers, musicians and artists congregated at Colla's Five & Dime Tap near the near East Side tanneries. Owners Marcella and Francie Colla waterfalled giant tappers and served "Texas and Shoes," their signature hamburger and shoestring potatoes. The place was popular, especially since a glass of wine was five cents, a mug of beer was ten cents and cocktails peaked at twenty-five cents. A hungry cub reporter from the Hearst-owned *Milwaukee Sentinel* could buy a hard-boiled egg for a nickel or a ham sandwich basted in beer sauce, sparked with ring of pineapple studded with cloves—all for ten cents.[39]

Checking out leftovers from a night's fun in the mid-1930s, Harold Gauer (right), Bill Williams and Robert Bloch consider the woes of their frivolity. Bloch went on to be the writer of *Psycho*, the basis for the frightening film of the same name by Alfred Hitchcock. *Photo courtesy of Harold Gauer estate and Precision Process/Urge Press.*

In the 1940s, Barney and Emmet Frederick managed the tiny Wayside Inn in a downtown alley at Number 1 Northwestern Lane, frequented by journalists, lawyers and others of similar ill-repute. Emmet died in the South Pacific during World War II, but Barney kept plugging away for another decade. Regulars kept track of their own drinks by marking their names on whichever liquor bottle they favored.

Smiley's Tavern on Vliet Street put a different twist on the saloon theme, specializing in wine, Gauer recalled. "He had barrels of them laid on their sides in tier and tapped from the barrelhead with spigots. There was a choice of white port, tokay, muscatel, zinfandel, claret and a dozen other varieties, all tasting remarkably like sweet soda pop needled with spirits. A glass was five cents, and a gallon could be had for sixty-nine cents, but drinkers had to bring their own jug."[40]

Other popular taverns in the 1930s included Jordan's Café at Plankinton and Wells, noted for its marvelous mahogany bar and hearty servings of excellent pea soup. At the Big Stein, also on Plankinton, drinkers could throw their peanut shells on the floor and sip their beer from frosty stone mugs. At Wendelin Kraft's cocktail bar on Jefferson Street, fresh milk was available for teetotaling Socialists off duty from city hall. Six-time mayor Dan Hoan and eventual mayor Frank Zeidler, both good, squeaky-clean Social Democrats, were among those who gathered there to talk strategy with their cronies. The Sixteenth Ward Democratic Organization met regularly at Gaynor's Tavern on Twenty-seventh and Wells, while the Twenty-sixth Ward diehards wandered to different watering holes, usually "with more beer on the way… leaving things pretty hysterical."[11]

Scribe and pub-crawler Gauer died in 2009, leaving much of his estate to the Milwaukee Press Club, of which he was a lifelong member. The organization is the longest continuously operating press club in North America. After a series of moves, it is now tucked into the first floor of the Fine Arts Building at 137 East Wells Street, across the street from the ornate Pabst Theater. Since 1885, the press organization has collected signatures of notable personalities, from presidents to burlesque queens. Many of the autographs are exhibited on the walls of the club's venerable Newsroom Pub, where the city's advertising and public relations crowd hangs with staffers from nearby governmental offices and area journalists. Gauer's donation was used for scholarships, programs and related activities sponsored by the club.

The Newsroom Pub is now managed by the Safe House, which opened in the lower level of the Fine Arts building in 1966. The latter nightspot is secreted behind an entry to what is mysteriously called International Exports, Ltd. A password is needed to get in the narrow entrance from the Front Street alley. The haven is a favorite of off-duty, real-life Secret Service agents and other security types accompanying major dignitaries, including whoever is the occupant of the White House at that time visiting Milwaukee. Two secret passages connect the Newsroom Pub and the Safe House, allowing for quick getaways after a round or two.[12]

Bowling, beer and Milwaukee go together. Brew City's Holler House is the oldest certified bowling alley in the United States and contains the two oldest sanctioned lanes in the nation. Both alleys are still tended by real, live pinsetters. In 2006, the tavern was rated by *Esquire* magazine as one of the best bars in America.[13] Holler House was opened by "Iron Mike" Skowronski as Skowronski's Tavern on September 13, 1908. By 1912, the price of a roast beef sandwich had soared to a quarter. Allegedly during Prohibition, liquor was stored under a baby's crib in the backroom, supposedly because the local police wouldn't look there and risk needing to calm a screaming little one. Skowronski's son, Gene, and daughter-in-law, Marcy, took over in 1952, renaming it Gene and Marcy's, the latter managing the bar after her husband's death. About 1975, the place was nicknamed "Holler House" by a neighbor. Holler House sells only bottled beer, with the exception of Schlitz in a can. Among its notable keglers and gutter-ballers were professional bowler Earl Anthony, who amassed a total of forty-three titles on the Professional Bowlers Association tour; guitarist Joe Walsh; actress Traci Lords; and Frank Deford, a *Sports Illustrated* senior writer and National Public Radio commentator.[14]

Koz's Mini Bowl at 2078 South Seventh Street is another iconic bar-bowling alley. With its four short lanes for duckpin bowling, Koz's is one of the last remaining such sports bars in the country. The balls used in duckpin bowling weigh two to four pounds each, have a maximum regulation diameter of five inches and don't have finger holes. Local kids still set the pins at Koz's, much as was done in the 1880s at the height of the game's popularity.[15]

The Landmark Lanes, in the basement of the Oriental Theater, dates from 1927, when the Theater and Bensinger's Recreation were built on the site of the former Farwell Station, a horse, mule and streetcar barn. When Prohibition gasped its last breath, the wild and woolly Club Silver opened in Bensinger's. The place was sold to United Artists in the early 1950s, making it the only theater in the nationwide chain complemented by a bowling alley. In 1973, Pritchett's Jazz Oasis swung wide open there, featuring formidable guitarist George Pritchett. Over the next several years, the room featured local and national jazz performers. Demonstrating its lure for all types of Milwaukeeans, in 1979, the Lanes hosted the first Holiday Invitational Tournament, the city's premiere gay and lesbian bowling tournament. In 1980, the Jazz Oasis reopened as a second bar and dart room. In 2002, then-owners the Pritchett brothers sold the theater and lanes to New Land Enterprises, with Slava Tuzhilkov assuming a majority position. As the Landmark approached its centennial, famous visitors included feminist Gloria Steinem, numerous athletes and dozens of politicians looking forward to its beer pitcher specials and Bloody Marys. Entertainers performing in the bar area have ranged from the Dixie Chicks to Todd Rundgren and Nora Jones.[46] These days, moviegoers at the upstairs Oriental can purchase wine to sip while viewing the latest Academy Award nominee.

Hooligan's Super Bar at 2017 East North Avenue has been a fixture on the East Side scene since 1936. It now boasts twelve big-screen televisions and

92

more than thirty micro and import drafts, plus the usual selection of local brews. In the old days, Hooligan's was more of a shot-and-beer place than a sports scene. In one incident in those revered days, a motorcyclist allegedly maneuvered his big iron up the front steps of the triangle-shaped building, roared through the bar, grabbed up a stein of frothy beverage and rumbled full throttle out the back door. The procedure was done with finesse, without running over any patrons or knocking over a stool. According to the story, a number of the diehard patrons didn't even notice.[17]

Tiny, but fabled nonetheless, Wolski's is Milwaukee's longest-running family-owned bar, found at 1836 North Pulaski Street. "I Closed Wolski's" is a catch phrase printed on vibrantly colored bumper stickers found worldwide, from Hollywood to armored Humvees in Baghdad's Green Zone. Celebrating its 100th year in 2008 under the same family lineage, Wolski's remains a combination snug, caravansary, cozy front room, therapist's office and neighborhood hangout à la *Cheers* of television fame. Wolski's is owned by Dennis Bondar and his brothers, Mike and Bernie, who grew up and still live nearby.

Their great-grandfather, Bernard Wolski, a city fire hydrant inspector, opened his bar in 1908 at the foot of the steep Pulaski Street hill a few blocks north of Brady Street. The year before, the Polish émigré moved the former retail store there from another lot, using horses and roller logs. Over the ensuing generations, a succession of great-uncles and other relatives ran the bar, with assorted children, spouses and cousins also working there. The tavern was taken over by Michael and Bernard in 1973, when Dennis was a teenager. He became a partner when in his twenties. All work the bar, taking various shifts and dividing managerial duties.

As with many longtime Milwaukee bars, Bondar retained a dedicated help staff, such as longtime bartenders Paul Johnson and Angela Cooper and doorman Tony Miller, each of whom has been there for more than a decade. Those familiar faces, plus the general geniality packed into about one thousand square feet, means Wolski's is the quintessential Milwaukee tavern. Part of the basement still has its original dirt floor, where the cool temperatures there make for perfect beer and wine storage. Old boxing and political posters, photos of Wolski's fans in exotic ports of call and other memorabilia paper the walls.

A good bartender needs a good ear, a feature that retains patrons of all collar colors, whether blue, white, pink or other. Over the years, the brothers have become fast friends with folks such as Eddie Lebanowski, a retired postman who died in 2007 at age ninety-two. For decades twice a week,

Lebanowski and his wife, Gertie, walked to Wolski's for his favorite drink, a whiskey press. Over the years, thousands of Milwaukeeans and assorted star guests, such as the fabled Father Guido Sarducci (comedian Don Novello of *Saturday Night Live* notoriety) have counted Wolski's among their favorite watering holes.

The "I Closed Wolski's" phrase came about in the 1970s, when Mike's rugby-playing pals flocked to Wolski's to replay matches over plenteous beverages. Late one night, a patron suggested the motto, and it immediately took off, with Wolski's ubiquitous bumper stickers sprouting like mushrooms around the world. Friends and patrons still carry them on military tours of duty, on vacations and business trips. The tavern also has the de rigeur T-shirts and even lady's thongs, all designed and produced by longtime friend, John Behling of Oostburg's Mount'n Screenery. Obviously, such items show up in the most interesting places, indeed.

Since none of the unmarried Bondar partners has any kids, although Michael and Bernard have longtime girlfriends, the bar ownership may eventually pass on to one of their three sisters' children.[18] Always promotions-minded, Wolkski's did have one major roadblock in its history.

The Milwaukee Police Department began aggressively enforcing tavern capacity laws in 2007, judging overcrowding by square footage, number of exits and number of restrooms. Concerned about the growing popularity of its annual pub crawl, which could have made it an easy mark for a fine, Wolski and several other area bars canceled their ever-growing spring event that year, when the participant count began hitting the thousands.[19] All has since been resolved, and life happily proceeds as before.

The building housing Fitzgibbons' Pub at 1127 North Water Street has another illustrious history, housing what many consider to be the city "oldest gin joint." The structure was built in the late 1800s for Weisel's Sausage factory. When that company moved to a larger facility, the building was converted into a bar shortly after the end of Prohibition and subsequently housed a number of taverns under different names ever since. Over the years, it was noted for being "the real deal for real men who drink real drinks." Daniel Fitzgibbons opened it as Fitzgibbons' Pub in 1998, boasting Milwaukee's only outdoor pool table, plus loads of free advice and criticism and, thank heavens, indoor bathrooms. According to Fitzgibbon, "If you want blended drinks, go somewhere else. We don't have a blender."[50]

Mike Roman loves his beer—and history. He has plenty of both at his Roman's Pub, at 3473 South Kinnickinnic Avenue, which was originally a stagecoach stop and roadhouse dating to 1885. A great neighborhood saloon, this long-ago speakeasy featured a regularly rotating roster of up to thirty often hard-to-find new draft micros on a regular basis. The pub was owned by the same family from 1919 until purchased in 1978 by Mike Roman, who began specializing in craft beers in the mid-1990s and then added cigars and wines to his stock. He had no problem with the state's smoke-free legislation, either. Puffers sit out on his heated back deck and order beverages through a window, "just like Dairy Queen." Only peanuts, chips and assorted snacks are available, but Roman allows food carry-ins and even provides the paper plates. Decor remains eclectic, with loads of beer memorabilia, old advertising and drinking-related paraphernalia. Although the building can be easily missed on a quick drive-by, the elaborate Paulaner Munchen bracket with its Romans' Pub signage hanging above the entrance is the landmark.[51]

What's a city without its Irish bars? Among those in the Milwaukee area claiming a Celtic link are Mo's Irish Pub, Judge's, Brocach Irish Pub, Trinity Three Irish Pubs, the Black Rose, Halliday's, the Blackthorn, Murphy's, McBob's and Caffrey's. Some are more faux Irish than others, but the *craic*—the good times—still roll on regardless of owner ethnicity and number of televisions on the walls.

Milwaukee has long had a heritage of Gaelic drinking establishments, particularly in the era of the Civil War, in what was then the rough, tough, "Bloody" Third Ward. With its grogshops and dives, the neighborhood ranged along the Milwaukee River and was noted for being one of the toughest districts in the city. In the mid-1800s, Chief William Beck's beat cops, brawny lads such as the iron-knuckled Tom Shaugnessey, earned their thirty dollars a month the hard way. They were expected to whomp any miscreants as much as necessary before hauling them off to the hoosegow.[52]

Among the early Irish tavern keepers was John McCarthy, who became proprietor of the famed Union House after a stint as a Great Lake sailor and Civil War veteran. Ireland-born John Curran ran a bar and billiard parlor on Lincoln Avenue, while Richard Casey, who launched the Milwaukee chapter of the Ancient Order of Hibernians in the late 1880s, operated a saloon at 67 North Third Street. Tom Doorley (sometimes spelled Doerly or even Doerley) operated a bar at 196 Erie Street. His father, Martin, was Milwaukee harbormaster and a color sergeant in the Union Guards who drowned in the sinking of the *Lady Elgin* steamship on Lake Michigan on September 8, 1860.[53]

That sinking was a disaster for Milwaukee's Irish community and changed the city's ethnic face. A state historical plaque near the Irish

Pub at 124 North Water Street is not far from where the *Lady Elgin* sailed on its ill-fated voyage. The pub building dates from 1904 as a Pabst tied house and workingman's hotel, with a Pabst logo still seen on the south wall. The structure also once housed a dockers' bar called the Captain's Table and for thirty years was home to the city's longest-running gay bar. The Irish Pub opened its doors in 2007.[54]

Each year, the pub regulars raise a toast to the long-deceased who drowned on the doomed *Lady Elgin*. There were nearly four hundred confirmed deaths, making it the greatest open-water loss of life in the history of the Great Lakes. Among the dead were brewer John P. Engelhart; Lacy Lasky, the *Elgin*'s bartender; and a number of Milwaukee's best-known, politically connected tavern keepers and saloon owners.[55] The 150th anniversary of the *Lady Elgin* sinking was marked on September 8, 2010, with the premiere of *A Rising Wind*, presented by the Damned Theatre at the Best Place Tavern in the renovated Pabst Brewery complex.[56]

Legendary Christopher (Kit) Nash initially operated a pub in his hometown of Dublin, where he had also operated a bar. Coming to the United States, Nash opened Nash's Irish Castle, at 1328 West Lincoln Avenue, in the mid-1970s. Now a Mexican bar/restaurant, Nash's was home to numerous Irish-born and wannabes. It was a snug haven in which to meet, sip beer and listen to live music; it was also one of the first places in town to offer vinegar with its french fries in fine Gaelic tradition. With his wife, Josie, running the operation from behind the bar, Nash held court from a stool at the far end of the room. At closing time, everyone knew it was time to go when Nash stately rose from his perch and announced, "Have you no feckin' homes to go to?" Another admonition was offered to ensure a successful entrepreneurship, "Own your own building and have no partners."[57]

Danny and Helen O'Donoghue were proud of the restaurant and expansive bar they operated on West Blue Mound Road from 1986 to 1996. Coming to Milwaukee from Killarney in 1949, O'Donoghue owned a popular State Street pub for a number of years even while working as a laborer and foreman at the nearby Miller Brewing Company. O'Donoghue partnered for a time with his uncle, Big Jim Hegarty, who also owned nine other bars in Milwaukee since his first pub in 1939. A formidable figure who kept a baton under his backbar in case of trouble, Cork native Hegarty came to the United States in 1926, after fighting and being wounded in the hand during in the Irish Civil War. His final bar, located near Marquette University and a popular hangout for decades of law students, was called Flanigan's for years before Hegarty bought it in 1972.

Ray Flynn (seated at right), three-time mayor of Boston, dropped in at Kit Nash's Irish Castle on Milwaukee's South Side to encourage support for Democratic presidential candidate Bill Clinton. Flynn eventually went on to be Clinton's ambassador to the Vatican. Dublin-born Nash (seated at left) grinned as the pints circulated. Joining Flynn and Nash were then Milwaukee major John Norquist and former alderman Kevin O'Connor. *Photo by John Alley, courtesy of the* Irish American Post.

Big Jim died of a heart attack in his tavern in 1981, and the space was then sold, closing in 2010 after the then-owner filed for bankruptcy. Yet carrying on the family tradition, Danny and Helen O'Donoghue's son, Jamie, owns O'Donoghue's Irish Pub in Elm Grove, still offering lively music sessiúns and strenuous rounds of set dancing.[58]

Milwaukee's Irish bars have not only been watering holes but literary and artistic centers as well. In the early 1990s, Tom Connelly's late, lamented Black Shamrock on Milwaukee's East Side and Cecilia's Pub, managed by Kerry Wiedemann on South Second Street, attracted large crowds for music, poetry readings and theatrical presentations.[59]

Owner Rip O'Dwanny has the corner on Irish inns. Among them is the County Clare, which opened in 1996 at 234 North Astor Street. O'Dwanny's also owns 52 Stafford in Plymouth, where each room is named after an Irish personality, and St. Brendan's Inn in Green Bay. For a number of years, O'Dwanny also operated the Castledaly Manor House in Athlone, County Westmeath. The inn was located not far from Locke's Distillery, an Irish institution that traces its roots back to 1757. O'Dwanny's Milwaukee

Josie Nash of Nash's Irish Castle received a warm hug from Finbar MacCarthy, who first began singing in Dublin pubs at age twelve. Josie and her husband, Kit, were both born in Dublin and were among the principal advocates of Irish music in Milwaukee for decades. MacCarthy left Ireland in the early 1980s, performing in bars in the Canary Islands and then entertaining elsewhere throughout Europe. He eventually wound up in Wisconsin and opened his own bar in Saukville, a town just north of Milwaukee. *Photo by John Alley, courtesy of the* Irish American Post.

Danny and Helen O'Donoghue ran the show from the vantage point of their restaurant on Blue Mound Road from 1986 to 1996. O'Donoghue came to the United States from Killarney, County Kerry, in 1949 and became a laborer and foreman at Miller Brewing Company. He partnered for several years with his uncle, Big Jim Hegarty, a County Corkman who was then "chieftain" of the Milwaukee Irish bar owners. The O'Donoghues' son, Jamie, owns a bar in Elm Grove, a western Milwaukee suburb. *Photo by the author, courtesy of the* Irish American Post.

caravansary remains the "snug" for many of the city's Irish-born jackeens and bogtrotters. Dublin-born singer Barry Dodd is a regular performer.[60]

A native of County Cork and another nephew of the aforementioned Big Jim Hegarty, Derry Hegarty came to the States in 1965, taking over Feeney's for Fun Bar from Joe and Mae Feeney in 1972. Hegarty's sister, Margaret, ran the nearby Mr. Guiness [*sic*] Tavern for a number of years, a happy place that was the initial planning base for the Milwaukee Irish Fest, now the world's largest Irish cultural event. Greeting guests for years at the bar rail was Muldoon, Hegarty's longtime St. Bernard pal, known for

There's a Tavern in the Town

Owner Tom Connolly stands outside his Black Shamrock pub, a feature of Milwaukee's East Side bar and arts scene in the early 1990s. Connolly regularly hosted Celtic-themed theater presentations, poetry readings, photo exhibits and music in his place, a block north of the entertainment hub along East North Avenue. *Photo by the author, courtesy of the* Irish American Post.

Cary (Rip) O'Dwanny received his nickname for his prowess in batting baseballs as a youngster on Milwaukee's East Side, not far from where he operates the County Clare guesthouse. The County Clare, which opened in 1996, remains a social center for Milwaukee's émigré Irish community. Long active in the bar, restaurant and hotel business, O'Dwanny first renovated the 52 Stafford, an Irish inn in Plymouth, Wisconsin, the oldest continually operating hotel in the state. He then moved on to open other hospitality facilities, including St. Brendan's Inn in Green Bay and Castledaly, a restored manor in Athlone, County Westmeath, Ireland. *Photo by Dan Hintz, courtesy of the* Irish American Post.

The rousing Irish band, 180 & the Letter G, performed in 1998 in the County Clare. *From left*: fiddler Ed Paloucek, flautist Brett Lepshutz, Dan Beimborn and Marine Doyle on the *bodhrán*, an Irish drum. *Photo by John Alley, courtesy of the* Irish American Post.

his affection for beer. An adjoining hall has long been a major hot spot for political fundraisers and other rousers, whether Veterans for Peace or the Emerald Society. Hegarty remodeled the banquet area with $96,000 from winnings he garnered at a Las Vegas slot machine.

Hegarty's remains a top-rated neighborhood pub, happily ensconced on the holiest corner in Milwaukee. His building at 5328 West Bluemound Road is across the street from Calvary Cemetery, where many victims of the *Lady Elgin* sinking and other notable Irish are buried. It is also a block to the east of St. Vincent Pallotti Parish. One regular Hegarty patron was Archbishop Timothy M. Dolan, who had been Milwaukee prelate before heading to New York City and St. Patrick's Cathedral pulpit in 2009. The archbishop regularly used Hegarty's banquet room for his "Theology on Tap" speaker series.[61]

When the bar owner died of cancer in April 2011, Milwaukee's Irish waked him in fine style at St. Vincent Pallotti, with an honor guard from the Wisconsin Shamrock Club and many friends from the Emerald Society, Ancient Order of Hibernians and other Celtic organizations. He was subsequently buried at Cavalry Cemetery, overlooking Bluemound Road directly onto the front door of his bar.

Two sisters from Ireland, Eileen and Imelda, joined Hegarty's other siblings, Margaret and Joe, at the service. Another sister, Rose, was unable to make the trip because of her own illness. Memorial books brimmed with notable names, including Mayor Tom Barrett, Julie Smith, Annie Lynch, John Reilly, Mike Cassidy, Scott McNulty, Dr. Dennis Dwyer, pundit Wayne Youngquist, Irish Fest "poster girl" Veronica Ceszynski, Mike Driscoll, Dennis Murphy and Ed and Betty Mikush. Loads of Brennans, Farleys, Coffeys, Glynns, Phelans and Conleys admired the displayed proclamations, certificates and plaques honoring the iconic Gaelic pub keeper. Hegarty's invitation to President Bill Clinton's inauguration and numerous photos of him with other political leaders were also exhibited.

Derry's brother Joe Hegarty emigrated from Drinach, County Cork, in 1965 and was almost immediately drafted in the United States Army. He served as an E-4 in the artillery, fighting in the Central Highlands of Vietnam. Discharged in 1968, Hegarty went on to get a business degree from the University of Wisconsin–Milwaukee and opened the Glocca Morra Pub near the Marquette University campus in 1976. The bar had formerly been a metal-studded biker hangout called the Black Spider. The building's storied history was lost when it was purchased from Hegarty and subsequently razed by Marquette for another university structure.[62]

Annie James, hailing from the rough-and-tumble Liberties district in Dublin, opened the original Dubliner bar in Walker's Point on Milwaukee's South Side back in the 1990s. She acted as mother hen to dozens of Irish entertainers visiting Milwaukee on tour who usually stopped in for a pint and tunes. An upscale, streamlined gastro pub also called the Dubliner opened at 124 West National Avenue, around the corner from James's original pub, which had been shuttered for several years. Jerry Stenstrup, owner of nearby Steny's Bar, revived the Dubliner name in 2010. He does an admirable traditional Irish breakfast with bangers (sausages), rashers (bacon) and black and white pudding.[63]

Always the center of lively partying for all the participating Irish societies in the St. Patrick's Day parade, the Irish Cultural & Heritage Center at 2133 West Wisconsin Avenue hosts year-round music *súns* and intricate ceili dancing. Located in the historic Grand Avenue Congregational Church, the facility sponsors concerts, art exhibits, classes and other family-oriented activities. Quinlan's Bar is the center's heart, offering one of the best pours of Guinness in town.[64]

Two other bars retain the flavor and charm of a real Irish getaway. Packy Campbell grew up on the outskirts of Dublin and has a life-long love affair with Irish sports. On any given day, a visitor might see hurling or gaelic football on the "telly" in Packy's Irish Pub at 4068 South Howell Avenue. The place fills with local rugby and soccer players eager for a home where

Above, left: Annie James hailed from the Liberties neighborhood in Dublin and subsequently named her Milwaukee bar after her native city when it opened in 1996. The Dubliner was noted for its music *sessiuns* and for hosting numerous Irish dignitaries and traveling entertainers. Here, James and her daughter, Peggy, play with their dog Bailey. The Dubliner closed in the early 2000s. *Photo by author, courtesy of the* Irish American Post.

Above, right: The Irish Cultural and Heritage Center of Wisconsin was formerly the Grand Avenue Congregational Church, built in 1887. Its auditorium seats thirteen hundred persons and holds one of Wisconsin's largest pipe organs. Quinlan's Pub there is open for sing-alongs, Irish music *sessiuns* and informal gatherings of friends. In 1986, the facility was listed on the National Register of Historic Places. *Photo by author, courtesy of the Irish American Post.*

talk gets beyond the Green Bay Packers' omnipresent green and gold chatter. Paddy's Pub at 2339 North Murray Avenue is run under the keen eyes of Patty Egan, whose grandparents hail from County Sligo, and those of her husband, Woody, a burly ex-undercover cop. Both hold court behind the tappers and keep the *craic* ever lively. Patty is ever augmenting the decor with a collector's eye, gathering all sorts of gee-gaws to adorn the walls and ceilings. Each return visit to Paddy's showcases something new. Bowls of M&Ms and peanuts are bar fodder, and Jameson is the whiskey of choice.[65]

Prohibition's Hammer

We are going to make Milwaukee drier than the Sahara Desert.
—Nelson White, chief prohibition officer[1]

Almost as long as there has been alcohol in Wisconsin, there have been various movements to halt drinking, or at least temper overindulgence. The state's first official temperance society was formed in Green Bay in 1835, probably in reaction to cavorting soldiers on leave from Fort Howard.[2] On February 13, 1840, the Wisconsin Temperance Society met to deliver the following mission: "We the undersigned, do agree, that we will not use intoxicating liquors as a beverage, nor traffic in them—that we will not provide them as an article of entertainment, or for persons in our employment—and that, in all suitable ways we will discountenance their use throughout the community."

Temperance advocates in Milwaukee produced the state's first reform newspaper, the *Wisconsin Temperance Journal*. This premiere issue, printed in April 1840, featured the constitution of the society, meeting minutes and articles related to what the publishers saw as the problem of alcohol. Despite backing by some of Milwaukee's most prominent citizens, the paper was short-lived.[3]

But reformers did not give up easily. In 1842, Caleb Wall, a flatlander from Springfield, Illinois, rode into town to establish a temperance hotel, refitting the old Milwaukie [sic] House at Main and Wisconsin Streets "with all the modern accessories of comfort." However, according to house rules, guests had to be tucked inside by 10:00 p.m. But frontier habits were hard to break, with guests regularly resorting to ladders and ropes to get back into their rooms after hours. After all, Milwaukee was a town where there was no curfew for *gemütlichkeit*. Despite Wall's excellent larder, the piano for hymns and a house combo made up of the African American barber, cook and kitchen staff, the out-of-towner sold his place at auction in 1844 and moved on, seeking more savable souls elsewhere.[1]

March is the Green Month, ostensibly honoring St. Patrick and St. Bridget, Ireland's two patron saints. The first St. Patrick's parade in Milwaukee was a procession in 1843, headed by Father Martin Kundig, a German priest who was the second pastor of St. Peter's Church. The event was organized by the Wisconsin Temperance Society, with the genteel idea of leading Milwaukee's thousands of newly immigrated Irish to "sober respectability." Obviously, that particular non-drinking effort needed additional fine-tuning, and subsequent parades over the generations have loosened up.[5] Yet Kundig didn't saunter alone. Hundreds of local Milwaukee Irish had already "taken the pledge," a cause advanced by Father Theobald Mathew, later honored by a statue in Dublin's O'Connell Street. Subsequently, plenty of Gaels joined Kundig in that first St. Pat's procession, numbering about three thousand persons. The parade remained downtown through 1975, until major bridge repair and construction necessitated a route change. Since then, the parade has been held at various locales in the city, including in the old Polish bastion of Mitchell Street, now primarily a Hispanic neighborhood. It was also held on North Avenue on Milwaukee's far West Side, returning to its original downtown route in 2002.[6]

Despite beer's popularity among Wisconsin immigrants and the rapid growth of breweries, alcohol consumption became a controversial issue in Wisconsin. The Sons of Temperance Grand Division organized in Milwaukee in 1848, pushing for prohibition laws. Wisconsin's burgeoning ethnic population naturally objected to these attempts. However, in 1872, the legislature passed the Graham Law, which held tavern owners responsible for selling liquor to known drunks.[7] The Graham Law was replaced the following year by a law that encouraged local municipalities to work with taverns to prevent drunkenness, a measure that stayed in place for the next forty or so years.

The roots of the temperance were complicated in Wisconsin, becoming more than merely a battle between drinkers and nondrinkers. Atavists feared the growing influence of "those outsiders," émigrés who remained attached to their cultural roots, including drinking beer, using their Old World languages and even their choice of religion, notably papist Catholicism. This combination made for a perfect cultural storm during World War I, when anti-German sentiment was especially strong.[8]

Anti-alcohol forces in the state slowly gained the upper hand, despite intensive lobbying efforts by breweries, distilleries and their ancillary businesses. Wisconsin watched carefully as other states enacted ordinances prohibiting alcohol within their borders; however, the Anti-Saloon League and other moralists felt even that was not enough. The temperance groups complained that passage of the Webb-Kenyon Law of 1913 lacked the national bite that was considered necessary. This federal ruling prevented liquor shipments from a wet state into a dry one.[9] The league raised millions of dollars to counter ads by the breweries, plus contributed thousands to the political campaign of office-seekers who would support its platform. Their efforts paid off in the 1916 election, when numerous "dry" candidates were elected across the country. The enthusiastic new Congress was ready to push the Anti-Saloon League's agenda and quickly did just that with a series of legislative steps, culminating with the House of Representatives passing the Eighteenth Amendment on December 18, 1917. It then needed to be ratified by the states.[10]

Finally, on January 16, 1919, the Eighteenth Amendment was ratified by thirty-six of the forty-eight states. Wisconsin approved the ruling by a vote of nineteen to eleven in the state senate on January 16, 1919, and fifty-eight to thirty-five in the House on the following day, making it the fortieth state to do so.

The legislation declared:

> *Section 1. After one year from the ratification of this article the manufacture, sale, or transportation of intoxicating liquors within, the importation thereof into, or the exportation thereof from the United States and all territory subject to the jurisdiction thereof for beverage purposes is hereby prohibited.*
>
> *Section 2. The Congress and the several States shall have concurrent power to enforce this article by appropriate legislation.*
>
> *Section 3. This article shall be inoperative unless it shall have been ratified as an amendment to the Constitution by the legislatures of the several States, as provided in the Constitution, within seven years from the date of the submission hereof to the States by the Congress.*
>
> *Section 4. Cases relating to this question are presented and discussed under Article V.*

Enforcement Cases produced by enforcement and arising under the Fourth and Fifth Amendments are considered in the discussion appearing under the those Amendments.[11]

Minnesota Republican Andrew Volstead introduced the National Prohibition Act, the enabling legislation for the amendment, in the House as H.R. 6810 on June 27, 1919. The Volstead Act passed the House on July 22, 1919 (287–100, with 3 members stating "present") and passed the Senate with amendment on September 5, 1919. However, the bill was vetoed by President Woodrow Wilson on technical grounds because it also covered wartime prohibition. But the House overrode his veto on the same day, October 28, 1919, and the Senate did so one day later.[12]

The Volstead Act had three major provisions: 1) to prohibit intoxicating beverages; 2) to regulate the manufacture, production, use and sale of high-proof spirits for other than beverage purposes; and 3) to ensure an ample supply of alcohol and promote its use in scientific research and in the development of fuel, dye and other lawful industries and practices, such as religious rituals.[13]

Hardy Milwaukee drinkers gathered for a "last call" only a few days before Prohibition shut down the city's brewing and distilling industries. *Photo courtesy of Miller/Coors-Milwaukee.*

Prohibition's Hammer

The Eighteenth Amendment took effect on midnight, January 16, 1920. Milwaukee immediately took an economic punch to the chin. At the end of World War I, there were nine operating breweries in Milwaukee directly employing some sixty-five thousand workers. They accounted for $35 million annual tax revenue for the city. Ancillary services included barrel makers, glass manufacturers and related businesses. When the taverns shuttered, the city lost $500,000 in license fees during each of the fourteen years of Prohibition.[14]

Much of the turmoil surrounding Prohibition has been richly outlined by Richard C. Crepeau in his 1967 thesis for Marquette University and Jeffrey Lucker in his 1968 University of Wisconsin thesis on the subject.[15] As they indicated in their writings, it was obvious that there were plenty of challenges to enforcing the law, even as Milwaukeeans began converting saloons to ice cream parlors and bar taps to soda fountains. Perhaps ninety-year-old Jeremiah Quin, an early Milwaukee teetotaling settler, said it best when he bemoaned the law:

> *I am opposed to the present form of prohibition. The manner in which attempts are made to enforce this law is offensive to me as it must be to every man of spirit. From the observations of political movements for more than half a century, I conclude that this form of prohibition will not continue; it is producing a daily increasing reaction against the policies in force. It is the manner, not the morals that is offensive.*[16]

Brewers needed to rise to the challenge. Early on, well before the Eighteenth Amendment's passage, Schlitz president Joseph Uihlein was prescient enough to note that the growing temperance movement throughout the country was bound to eventually adversely affect the company's operations. Subsequently, he urged the brewery and his family members who were stockholders to continue diversifying into non-brewing businesses. These efforts ranged from lumbering to the manufacturing of carbon electrodes for the steel industry. Since 1917, the company had already been producing a near beer called FAMO, which became a company profit center during the drought days of Prohibition.

Rather than duck the challenge, Uihlein's firm hand kept Schlitz viable from 1920 to 1933. He manufactured yeast, candy bars, malt syrup and Schlitz GingerAle. In 1920, the firm changed its name to Joseph Schlitz Beverage Company, but it was more commonly known as "Schlitz Milwaukee." Along with the corporate name change, the company slogan

A mock wake commemorates the advent of Prohibition in 1919. *Photo courtesy of Miller/Coors-Milwaukee.*

was modified to "Schlitz—the name that made Milwaukee famous." In 1921, Uihlein founded Eline's Inc., a chocolate and cocoa manufacturing company. The company's name was a phonetic word play on the "Uihlein" name. However, Eline was one of many companies that failed in the Great Depression following Prohibition, being liquidated in 1928.[17]

Milwaukee drinkers found many alternatives for their entertainment beverages during Prohibition, whether "coffin varnish," "giggle water," "hooch," "raisin juice" or quality liquor smuggled in from Canada or even secured with a "prescription" from a friendly doctor or druggist. When the man of the house said, "I have to see a man about a dog," everyone knew what he really meant. Such hide-and-seek games became a favorite pastime. But a drinker had to be careful. The first victim of poisoning from homemade booze was admitted to the city's Emergency Hospital on Saturday, January 17, 1920, the second day after the Volstead Act took effect.[18]

At first, federal Prohibition agents had a tough time enforcing the law within the city. In one incident at Liedertafel Hall, home of a German music society, an officer showed his identification. It took three Milwaukee cops to rescue the man from the angry crowd, who had tossed down their violas and beer mugs to confront the hapless fed.[19] Regularly working with state and local law enforcement, however, raids gradually grew more successful as Prohibition wore on, despite friction between agencies. In one night in 1921, three cars packed with lawmen raided more than fifty roadhouses and blind pigs on Milwaukee's environs, where illegal alcohol could readily be obtained. They confiscated so much evidence that they needed to pour their catch into the sewers.[20] Claiming to help, but more often getting in the way, were several civilian organizations, such as the Rotary Club, the Dry Law Enforcement League, the Anti-Saloon League and even the Ku Klux Klan, the latter vowing "to mop up the liquor and drive out of Milwaukee the gamblers and lewd characters who are leading our youth into sin."[21]

Some law enforcement officials were bagged for helping the rumrunners and bootleggers, whether by accepting bribes or even escorting caravans of trucks hauling illegal liquor. Among them were Nelson White, chief inspector for the state Prohibition office, and his assistant, Joseph Ray; Bert Herzog, head of federal Prohibition efforts for eastern Wisconsin; and numerous others.[22] It probably didn't help that former liquor dealer Charlie Schallitz was elected Milwaukee County sheriff in 1926 and served for two years during the height of Prohibition. Not known for his anti-beer sentiments, his cavalier motto was: "I don't want any dry votes." He also modestly asserted that he was the "best sheriff Milwaukee County ever had.[23] Milwaukee's Socialist mayor Dan Hoan, however, earnestly tried to enforce the Prohibition rulings but felt that the Eighteenth Amendment and the Volstead Act were the wrong methods for achieving the desired results.[24]

By 1926, it was obvious that Prohibition was not working out as planned. Milwaukee newspapers overflowed with stories of crime and corruption through the late 1920s: a soft drink parlor sold wine to West Division High School pupils on their lunch hour; senior citizens threw regular "orgies of dancing," fueled by bootleg alcohol at the St. Charles Hotel; "lovely daughters of Venus" and "flagons of potent, amber brew" enlivened a labor union rally; a raid uncovered whiskey hidden in a player piano; and when cops turned a faucet found at another place, gallons of moonshine whiskey flowed out from a buried hiding place.

Prominent businessmen, including bankers, Realtors, some of the city's top attorneys and residents of the "fashionable East Side Gold Coast," were busted in raids at the Valley Inn, the State Café, the Cape Horn Café, the Globe Hotel Bar, the North Shore Buffet, Kahlo's, the Tent, the Wayside Inn, the Kirby House Bar, Nick Heck's, the Little Old New York, the Monte

Carlo, the Moulin Rouge and numerous other Milwaukee restaurants and clubs. The arrests and raids became so numerous that they eventually barely rated mentions on the newspapers' inside pages.[25]

Despite the romanticism and the fact that many Milwaukeeans skirted the law just about any way they could, there was nothing funny about Prohibition's fallout. It wasn't long before rivals battled it out over the lucrative market in alcohol. Among the first murders attributed to the lawless conditions were those of hijacker Albert Sbeciali, shot seven times in the head; Sam (King of the Nightlife) Pick, murdered by a sawed-off shotgun blast; and Terry Kuzmanovic, a noted bootlegger and owner of the Te Kay Restaurant. The list of victims grew daily. Courtrooms were jammed. In three days in March 1927, "112 liquor violators were arraigned in federal district court, many of which necessitated jury trials."[26] But the government continued trying to stem the flow of booze. In 1928 alone, 29,000 gallons of alcohol were dumped, along with 81,000 gallons of beer, plus 465,000 gallons of mash destroyed, 186 stills smashed and 191 buildings padlocked for being secret warehouses or for selling alcohol out the back door.[27]

Yet a growing repeal movement had gained momentum by the late 1920s, fueled by editorials, speeches, sermons and meetings outlining Prohibition's moralistic bumbling. Milwaukee County supervisors and the city's Common Council both voted to repeal local Prohibition enforcement by 1929. Wisconsin senator John James Blaine, the twenty-fourth governor of Wisconsin and a former state attorney general, was a hardened political operative who saw that it was time to step forward. On December 6, 1932, Blaine submitted a resolution to Congress proposing the Twenty-first Amendment, which would annul the Eighteenth. Two months later, on February 21, 1933, the amendment was sent to the state governors. Meanwhile, the newly elected President Roosevelt asked Congress to modify the Volstead Act to provide for the sale of 3.2 percent beer. In nine days, Congress complied and legalized beer.[28]

On March 23, 1933, President Roosevelt signed into law the Cullen-Harrison Act, an amendment to the Volstead Act, to allow the manufacture and sale of light wines and the lighter "3.2 beer." When he signed the amendment relaxing the rules on the production of alcohol, the president remarked, "I think this would be a good time for a beer." Hearing this good news, Milwaukee brewers raced to get their products back in front of the public, with Schlitz and Miller among those cleaning and refurbishing equipment that had sat idle for more than a decade. All the breweries were eager to promote their beer, eyeing April 7, when the new law went into effect, eight months before the ratification of the Twenty-first Amendment.[29]

On April 17, 1933, Milwaukee celebrated the return of beer with twenty thousand revelers inside the old auditorium for a rousing Volkfest. Thousands more cavorted on the streets. Six bands played as the crowd roared *ein prosit!*—the German toast for happiness—and lifted mugs and bottles of their newly legal "near beer," including a Schlitz brand. The city's 1,776 taverns did a roaring business. Dozens of gleeful Milwaukeeans, including one woman in a mink coat, jumped on the front end of locomotive No. 8027 as it hauled the first trainload of quality real beer out of the Schlitz complex. A Schlitz company flag was affixed to the engine, proudly announcing the grand slogan, "Schlitz, The Beer That Made Milwaukee Famous."[30]

The new amendment was straightforward:

> *Section 1. The eighteenth article of amendment to the Constitution of the United States is hereby repealed.*
> *Section 2. The transportation or importation into every State, Territory, or possession of the United States for delivery or use therein of intoxicating liquors, in violation of the laws thereof, is hereby prohibited.*
> *Section 3. This article shall be inoperative unless it shall have been ratified as an amendment to the Constitution by conventions in the several States, as provided in the Constitution, within seven years from the date of the submission here of to the States by the Congress.*

Milwaukeeans breathed easier.[31]

Less than a year after the Twenty-first Amendment was submitted for ratification, the necessary thirty-sixth state ratified the amendment at 5:32 p.m. on December 5, 1933. At 7:00 p.m., President Roosevelt signed the proclamation ending Prohibition. Wisconsin had been the second state in line, ratifying the amendment way back, on April 25, 1933. The law would not officially take effect until December 15, but Milwaukeeans were already enjoying their foaming "head" start. Wisely, nobody in law enforcement paid any attention.

Beer Chasers

There was in the United States, in the beer age, no more delightful a city than Milwaukee, in which to spend a day, a year or a life.[1]

Milwaukee area chefs are a creative bunch, especially when considering cooking with a brewed or distilled beverage. Use of any product of local origin is another plus. The chefs love to list such selections on their menus, often presenting seasonal dishes made with beer or liquors from any of the city's producers.

One of the most interesting developments is Brian Frakes's deep-fried beer, a presentation launched in October 2010 at the Miller Time Pub in the Hilton Milwaukee Center. Frakes, the hotel's executive chef, developed his pretzel-ravioli pocket with a beer filling after learning of the possibilities of deep-frying beer. The technique originated with Mark Zable, a Belgian waffle concessionaire at the Texas State Fair.

According to the Texas Alcoholic Commission, fairgoers had to be twenty-one to sample it. Subsequently, the Miller Time Pub suggested that diners "please chew responsibly."

Frakes came up with his own recipe, which is served with a beer chaser, three dipping sauces, horseradish ale cream, nine-grain mustard and Wisconsin-made cheddar cheese.

For his basic ingredient, the chef selected the spicy, reddish-colored Staghorn Octoberbest beer for his recipe, brewed in the Swiss community of New Glarus, Wisconsin. However, any similar beer produced by a Milwaukee-based brewery should be an able substitute.

Frakes first froze the beer with gelatin to create what he calls "beer jewels," which are pressed into the dough. Frying takes about twenty seconds and returns the beer to its liquid state. Finishing the presentation, Frakes adds a sprinkle of rosemary fire salt.[2]

Milwaukee's Best Beer and Spirits Recipes

Carbonnade à la Flammande (Beef and Onions Braised in Beer)

Tom Peschong, executive chef, Riversite Restaurant

Tom Peschong, the executive chef at the Riversite Restaurant in Mequon since 1990, grew up in a cooking family, with six sisters, three brothers, mom Gertrude and dad Bob—all great cooks. Peschong received his formal culinary training in the Twin Cities and later helped launch Le Restaurant in Thiensville, where the late Journal-Sentinel restaurant critic Dennis Ghetto awarded him a coveted "Four Hats." He also worked at the old Fleur de Lis, as well as Jean Paul's and Brynwood Country Club. Peschong lives with his wife, Sheila, also a foodie, and seven-year-old son, Simon, in Cedarburg, Wisconsin.[3]

SERVES: SIX

4 tablespoons butter
2 pounds sweet onions (about four) thinly sliced
¼ pound Neuske's bacon (thickly sliced, then sliced into thick strips)
2–2½ pounds beef stewing meat (trimmed and sliced ¼-inch thick)
Salt and pepper to taste
2 tablespoons flour
2 tablespoons brown sugar
1 bottle Sprecher Black Bavarian beer
2 cups beef or veal stock
1 bay leaf
1 sprig fresh thyme (or 1 teaspoon dried thyme)
3 tablespoons flat leaf parsley (minced)

DIRECTIONS

1. Preheat over to 325 degrees Fahrenheit.
2. Heat butter in a large skillet over medium head and add onions. Cook slowly until lightly caramelized, stirring often. When ready, transfer to a side plate and hold until later.
3. Render bacon until crisp. Remove and set aside, leaving behind as much fat as possible.
4. Season beef with salt and pepper and cook as many pieces as possible at a time. Cook until all meat is nicely browned and then set aside, making sure that fat and oil remain behind.
5. Return skillet to flame and add flour and brown sugar, stirring until roux (sauce) is medium brown. Add Black Bavarian beer, stock and any accumulated juice from meat. Heat until lightly thickened and then add meat, onions, bay leaf and thyme.
6. Bake covered until meat is tender, about two hours. Let rest until any unwanted fat rises to the surface; skim and discard. Taste for seasoning and add salt and pepper as needed (to taste). Then finish with crispy bacon and parsley.
7. Serve with buttered noodles or red potatoes and chilled beer or a hearty red wine.

Truite de Riviere Farci Choux

(Roasted Rainbow Trout Stuffed with Sauerkraut)

Adam Siegel, executive chef, Bartolotta Restaurant Group

Milwaukeean Adam Siegel was named the 2008 Best Chef in the Midwest by the nationally acclaimed New York–based James Beard Foundation. The organization is named for cookbook author, teacher and champion of American cuisine James Beard, who died in 1985. Siegel was selected from among other area finalists after a rigorous culling process.

The award recognized Siegel for his culinary expertise in preparing French bistro cuisine at the Lake Park Bistro; he was cited for bringing a contemporary flair to the French preparation style of cooking. Siegel has more than one spatula in hand; he is also executive chef of Bacchus—A Bartolotta Restaurant.

Early in his career, Siegel studied under several other Beard winners in Chicago; San Francisco; Washington, D.C.; Italy; and France. A native of the Chicago area, Siegel graduated from the culinary school at Kendall College in Chicago.[1]

Serves: Four

4 ounces butter, unsalted
8 ounces sauerkraut, drained, rinsed and dried
1 each bay leaf
1 each garlic clove, sliced
3 each juniper berries
Salt and white pepper to taste
2 ounces Sprecher Special Amber
1 ounce white wine
3 ounces chicken stock
24 slices smoked bacon, ⅛ to ¼-inch thick
4 each rainbow trout, head off/pin bone out
1 ounce corn oil
8 ounces Shiitake mushrooms, stems removed and julienned
1 pound Yukon gold potatoes, b or c size, boiled and quartered
8 sprigs thyme

Directions

1. Place a sauté pan on medium heat and add about one ounce of butter. Add the sauerkraut, bay leaf, garlic, and juniper berries to the pan and season with salt and white pepper. Sauté and cook for a couple of minutes or until the kraut is hot.
2. Add the beer and wine and continue to cook until the liquid is reduced by half, then add the chicken stock. Cook until the chicken stock is reduced by half; remove from the heat; strain, reserving the liquid; and cool down the kraut. Remove all of the juniper berries and bay leaf from the sauerkraut.
3. On a piece of parchment or wax paper, lay out bacon slices lengthwise in groups of five, overlapping the slices by about ⅛ of an inch.
4. Take the trout and lay skin side down on a cutting board; trim any excess bones and fins, leaving the tail intact. Season with salt and pepper. Spread equal amounts of the sauerkraut in the center of each trout. Fold the trout closed so that the sauerkraut is in the belly of the trout.
5. Place each trout on a group of bacon slices. Roll the trout in the bacon so that it is completely covered and wrapped.

6. Place a nonstick sauté pan over medium heat and add the corn oil. Season the trout with salt and place in the pan with the seam side down. Sauté until the bacon renders and turns light brown; flip over and cook the other side. After the fish is brown on both sides, place the trout in a 350 degree Fahrenheit oven for about three to five minutes. Remove from the oven and allow to rest.

7. In the same pan with the bacon fat, add the mushrooms, potatoes and thyme. Sauté until golden brown, seasoning with salt. Place the trout on a plate with the vegetables, returning the pan to the heat. Add the reserved cooking liquid from the sauerkraut, finishing with the remaining butter. Pour the sauce around the trout and the vegetables.

Black and Tan French Toast

Thi Cao, former executive chef, Café Calatrava, Milwaukee Art Museum

Chef Thi Cao, executive chef at the Milwaukee Art Museum's trendy Café Calatrava, showcases his love of French, Asian, Spanish and Mediterranean cuisine. His vision for Café Calatrava was one where the food reflects the beauty of Milwaukee's signature building. He said his goal was to create a menu with a "wow" factor, while at the same time being affordable and approachable. He definitely succeeded.

Preferring to be called by his first name, pronounced "T," rather than "Chef," Cao was born in Vietnam and moved to Madison as an infant. His mother, Bichyen Tran, inspired his love of cooking. Cao raves about her pho, the century-old-plus national Vietnamese soup, hinting that her secret ingredients include saffron, star anise and orange.

Cao's interest in the food arts was also peaked by watching the cooking segments on Reading Rainbow at age nine. But his professional cooking career came much later. After receiving a business degree from the University of Wisconsin–Madison and working as a software quality engineer, he decided to follow his passion and enrolled in Pasadena's Le Cordon Bleu College of Culinary Arts in Los Angeles at the ripe old age of twenty-nine.

Since then, he has worked all over the world, his most recent job being a three-year stint as executive chef at Milwaukee's multiple award–winning Osteria del Mundo. His mentors include Michelin-magician chef Marc Fosh from the Palma de Mallorca in Spain and Chef George at the Cordon Bleu, who taught him the art of serenity in the kitchen. Cao takes pride in the calm, Zen-like atmosphere of his kitchen. He is also interested in greening up the workplace by composting and working with Milwaukee's urban fish and vegetable farmers' Sweet Water Organics.

Cao's menu was a foodie's delight. He used locally produced ingredients as often as possible, developing exquisite and often exotic combinations. His Steak and Potatoes was a signature item, pulling together a tenderloin, potato butter, roasted red pepper, artichoke and chocolate fig sauce. The Prosciutto Crab Melt had copious amounts of jumbo lump crab, and the Mustard Seed Chicken Sliders had pickled mustard seeds, free-range chicken and avocado mayo. Even the sometimes-lowly hot dog was elevated to a "haute" dog, made with never-tethered Strauss veal.[5]

SERVES: FOUR TO EIGHT

7 eggs
$^3/_4$ cup condensed milk
$1^1/_2$ cups milk
3 cups Sprecher Black Bavarian beer
$^1/_2$ teaspoon cinnamon
$^1/_4$ tablespoon vanilla extract
$^1/_2$ teaspoon nutmeg
1 loaf Texas toast, brioche or challah bread
2 tablespoons butter

DIRECTIONS

1. Beat the eggs and condensed milk to cream.
2. Slowly add the milk and beer while whisking constantly.
3. Add spices and mix thoroughly.
4. Heat a griddle on medium high.
5. Cut the bread in pieces about two fingers thick. Soak in the batter for 30 seconds on one side and then flip and let soak another 30 seconds.
6. Melt butter on the griddle and transfer the soaked bread to the hot griddle. Cook two to three minutes or until golden brown. Cook on the other side until golden brown.

Beer Chasers

Summer Senegalese, with Beer and Corn Pakoras

Sanford (Sandy) D'Amato, executive chef, Sanford Restaurant

Sanford D'Amato, owner of Sanford Restaurant in Milwaukee, graduated from the Culinary Institute of America in 1974 and stayed on for a one-year fellowship in the Escoffier Room. He then worked in various New York City restaurants throughout the 1970s. In 1980, he returned home to Milwaukee's John Byron's Restaurant, where he received national attention. In 1985, Food and Wine *magazine named D'Amato one of the top twenty-five "Hot New Chefs." In a 1998* Bon Appetit *feature article, he was touted as "one of the finest seafood chefs in the country." In 1988, he was selected as one of twelve national finalists in the American Culinary Gold Cup, Bocuse D'or.*

In 1992, D'Amato was one of twelve chefs in the nation to be personally chosen by Julia Child to cook for her eightieth birthday celebration in her hometown of Boston. In 1994, Sanford Restaurant was awarded the Fine Dining Hall of Fame award by Nation's Restaurant News *and received the DiRONA (Distinguished Restaurants of North America) Award. It has also consistently received the AAA-Four Diamond Award and the Four-Star Award from* Mobil Travel Guide. *After being nominated for six consecutive years by the James Beard Foundation, Sanford won the Perrier Jouet Best Chef Midwest Award in April 1996.*

He makes regular broadcast appearances and writes a food column for the Milwaukee Journal Sentinel *food section.*[6]

2 tablespoons grapeseed oil
2 teaspoons whole fennel seed
1 teaspoon whole kala jeera (black cumin seeds)
1 onion (10 ounces), peeled and cut in ½-inch pieces
2 stalks celery (4 ounces), washed and cut in ¼-inch pieces
1 carrot (5 ounces), peeled and cut in ¼-inch pieces
1 leek (4 ounces), cleaned and cut in ¼-inch pieces
6–7 large cloves garlic (1½ ounces), peeled and sliced thin
1 piece ginger root (3 ounces), washed, skin scraped off and sliced ¼-inch thick
2 Serrano peppers (¾ ounces), washed, stems removed and cut in ¼-inch pieces
2 bay leaves
2 teaspoons kosher salt
½ teaspoon fresh ground black pepper
2 tablespoons curry powder
6 cups low-sodium chicken stock

1 ripe mango (13–14 ounces) peeled, flesh cut off pit and diced large
2 tablespoons lime juice
Kosher salt and fresh ground black pepper to taste
1 cup good-quality plain yogurt

DIRECTIONS

1. Place a soup pot over medium heat. Add oil and when hot, add fennel seed and kala jeera.
2. Swirl and stir until fragrant, about one minute. Turn heat to medium low. Add next ten ingredients (after the kala jeera).
3. Stir, cover and let sweat without taking on any color, about 20 minutes, stirring regularly.
4. Add curry powder and stir one minute.
5. Add stock, bring up to a low simmer and simmer for 15 minutes covered.
6. Add mango, bring back up to a simmer, then carefully puree soup in small batches in a blender. Strain through a medium strainer.
7. Add lime juice and adjust seasoning with salt and pepper, then chill. To serve, place 2 tablespoons yogurt in center of each of 8 bowls.
8. Divide soup around yogurt and top with just-made crispy warm Beer and Corn Pakoras. Serve.

Beer and Corn Pakoras

SERVES: EIGHT

1 tablespoon whole butter
1 ear fresh corn, shucked and kernels removed (need ¾ to 1 cup)
Kosher salt and fresh ground black pepper to taste
½ cup, plus 2 tablespoons chickpea (gram) flour
¼ tablespoon baking powder
¾ teaspoon kosher salt
¼ teaspoon fresh ground black pepper
1 teaspoon ground fennel
⅛ teaspoon ground cayenne pepper
Microplaned zest of 2 limes
½ teaspoon sugar
2 tablespoons fine chiffonade of fresh mint leaves

3 tablespoons fine chopped chives
2½ cups oil for frying (peanut, corn, canola, etc.)
½ cup Lakefront Riverwest Stein beer

DIRECTIONS

1. Place an 8-inch nonstick sauté pan over high heat. Add butter and when dark brown but not burnt, add corn. Season lightly with salt and pepper, toss for 45 seconds and place on a plate to let cool.
2. In a mixing bowl, place flour, baking powder, ¾ teaspoon of salt, ¼ teaspoon of pepper, fennel, cayenne, lime zest, sugar, mint and chives.
3. Place oil in a 9- to 10-inch-diameter sauce pot and place over medium-high heat. Heat to 360 degrees Fahrenheit. Meanwhile, set up bowls as described previously.
4. Add beer to dry ingredients in bowl and whisk until smooth to form Pakora batter.
5. Mix in room temperature corn and, when oil is ready, carefully spoon in about 1 scant tablespoon portions of Beer and Corn Pakora batter in oil (not on top of one another so they don't stick together).
6. Let fry 2½ minutes per side until golden and crisp. Remove with slotted spoon, shake off excess oil and drain on absorbent paper. Keep warm.
7. Fry eight more. Place two warm Beer and Corn Pakoras in center of each bowl on top of yogurt and serve.

Sprecher Black Ninja Burger

Dan Kyle, 2010 First Place, Grilling With Beer Contest,

Wisconsin State Fair

Sprecher Brewing Company, the Wisconsin Beef Council (WBC) and Keg-a-Que annually join forces in the Wisconsin State Fair's Grilling with Beer competition. Second and third place winners each receive one case of Sprecher beverages, two Sprecher tour passes, a twenty-five-dollar certificate for beef from the WBC, a portable Keg-a-Que and other prizes.

The Grand Prize winner receives six cases of Sprecher beverages, two Sprecher Tour passes, a $200 certificate for beef from the Wisconsin Beef Council and a portable Keg-a-Que.[7]

BURGERS

½ cup teriyaki marinade
¼ cup Sprecher Black Bavarian Beer
2 pounds ground chuck
3 cloves garlic, chopped
⅓ cup chopped Sushi ginger
Chinese 5-Powder Spice (to season outside of burgers)
3 tablespoons butter
Ciabatta rolls

ASIAN BBQ BROCCOLI SLAW

3 cups broccoli slaw
3 tablespoons sesame oil
⅛ cup Sprecher Black Bavarian Beer
2 tablespoons rice wine vinegar
3 tablespoons sugar
4 tablespoons hoisin sauce
1 tablespoons soy sauce

DIRECTIONS

1. Add ½ cup teriyaki marinade and ¼ cup Sprecher Black Bavarian Beer to two pounds ground chuck. Chop two cloves of garlic and add to beef. Combine ingredients.
2. Make a thin patty, then add chopped ginger on top. Make a second thin patty and lay over top of the rest of the patty, making it into one patty. Season the outside of the burger patty with Chinese 5-Powder Spice. Grill to desired doneness.
3. In a small metal bowl, add one clove of garlic chopped and three tablespoons of butter. Melt butter and spread on sliced Ciabatta rolls.
4. Grill rolls for three to five minutes or until the rolls are toasted.
5. In a bowl combine broccoli slaw, sesame oil, Sprecher beer, rice wine vinegar, sugar, hoisin sauce and soy sauce. Mix well.
6. Place burger on Ciabatta roll and add Asian BBQ Broccoli Slaw over the top.
7. Enjoy the Sprecher Black Ninja Burger with more Sprecher Black Bavarian.

Author's Pear/Apple/Raspberry Liqueur

1 pound pears
2 Macintosh apples
1 cup red raspberries
3 cups Rehorst Vodka (Great Lakes Distillery)
1 cup sugar syrup
2 pinches nutmeg or cinnamon
2 pinches coriander seed
2 cloves

DIRECTIONS

1. To make sugar syrup, combine two cups of water with two cups of sugar. Stir until dissolved and boil for at least four minutes. Remove from heat and let cool.
2. Rinse fruit and cut pears and apples into slices, leaving on the skins. Place all the fruit in a large jar.
3. Pour in Rehorst Vodka and sugar syrup to cover fruit.
4. Add spices and remaining vodka and sugar syrup to fill jar. Seal tightly.
5. Shake jar once daily for three days to ensure even distribution of spices. Then set aside in a dark place for three months.
6. After three months, strain liquid to remove fruit, which can be saved for spreading atop a bowl of French vanilla ice cream. Let jar of liqueur stand and mellow in a cool, dark place for at least another three to six months before drinking. It gets smoother the longer it sits.

Marvelous Martini Suggestions from Great Lakes Distillery:

ABSINTHE MARTINI

2 ounces Rehorst Premium Milwaukee Vodka or Gin
½ ounce dry vermouth
¼ ounce Amerique 1912 Absinthe Verte

FRESH HERB MARTINI

3 ounces Rehorst gin
¼ ounce dry vermouth
3 sprigs fresh rosemary
1 sprig fresh thyme

PUMPKIN SPICE MARTINI

2 ounces Great Lakes Pumpkin Spirit
1 ounce heavy cream
½ ounce hazelnut liqueur
½ ounce Wisconsin maple syrup

Brewery Workers Unions

During the spring of 1886, the Milwaukee brewery workers and maltsters formed the Local 7953 chapter of the Gambrinus Assembly of the Knights of Labor. The new union asked the nine major Milwaukee breweries for an eight-hour workday, better pay and to allow the union in all the breweries. Rebuffed, most non-office brewery workers, except at the Falk Brewery, went on strike, joining workers at many other Milwaukee companies. On May 3, more than one thousand brewery workers marched to Falk to talk the workers there into joining them, and they did. By May 5, Republican governor Jeremiah Rusk sent the state militia to keep order in the city. In a confrontation at the North Chicago Rolling Mills in Bay View, the militia fired into a crowd of strikers, killing six persons. Eventually, they decided to concede on slight increases in pay, including an advance of $120 per year for each worker.[8]

Celebrating its 125th anniversary in 2011, Local Nine of the United Brewery Workmen was organized, as an affiliate of the American Federation of Labor after several years of labor strife that include a major multi-city strike in 1888. The local included almost every trade worker in the brewery world. Exempted were women who worked in the bottling house, spending up to ten hours a day applying labels to bottles at a starting wage of five cents an hour. In 1902, an attempt was also made to organize the women, but it stalled until Mary Harris Jones, a labor leader better known as "Mother Jones," arrived in Milwaukee to rally support for a union. In 1910, Local Nine began admitting women, getting them a minimum wage of six dollars a week. The men, on the other hand, were getting nine dollars.[9]

Spirits Publication

Suds, Wine & Spirits, Milwaukee's own quarterly newspaper featuring beer and beverage, is published by Jeff (Whispering Jeff) Platt, whose closing mantra is "Until We Party Again." For information, contact the publication at Box 1251, Milwaukee, WI 53201, www.sudswineandspirits.com.

The A. Gettelman Brewery rathskeller was refurbished in time for the 1937 gathering of the Master Brewers of America, which came to Milwaukee for its annual convention. Here, the brewery's Five O'Clock Club offers a toast with handmade copper boots of beer that Fritz Gettelman (far right) commissioned for the occasion. The guests included Dick and Fred Dunck, Louis Bajus, Joe Sausen and Julius Stimmler, who was Gettelman's brewmaster at the time. The three Dunck brothers (Pierre or "Pete," not pictured) rented offices from Gettelman for their cooperage firm. The Five O'Clock Club gifted Fritz Gettelman with Rex, his favorite springer spaniel. The caves that made up the rathskeller were first used by the Schweickhart Brewery for beer storage and cooling. *Photo courtesy of Nancy Moore Gettelman.*

Beer With Benefits

Surprise! Savoring a beer might be just what's needed as part of one's health regime. But the caveat emphasizes that this is a task undertaken only in moderation.

Beer in general, and in moderation, is beneficial for heart and cognitive function, both attributed to the beverage's alcohol content, said registered dietitian Joan Pleuss, a nutrition consultant to TOPS, the weight-loss support group. In addition, beer helps increase bone density because of its silicon content, she added.

Pleuss, also the bionutrition director for the Translational Research Unit at the Medical College of Wisconsin, indicated that ingredients such as wheat, yeast, malted barley and hops contribute to the B vitamin content of beer. Varieties of beer might offer different benefits, such as India Pale Ales, with their additional malt and hops, contributing to more silicon in the body and darker beers containing more antioxidants than lagers.

Pleuss added that a study done in the Netherlands shows that beer supposedly can decrease fibrinogen, a protein that contributes to blood clotting. It also decreased C-reactive protein, helping lower the risk of inflammation that leads to heart disease.

Keeping in mind the importance of not overdoing too much of a good thing, a glass or two of beer a day might be considered as much a part of a health regime as red wine. Pleuss, of course, emphasizes that women shouldn't exceed twelve ounces of beer per day and men twenty-four ounces.

There are several benefits to light or "low-cal" beer, Pleuss explains, especially since they do not have as many calories. "This variety of beer doesn't have the same risks for cancer, either," she explains, adding that it's the alcohol in beer that increases the risk for some types of cancer.

A number of organic beers have arrived in the marketplace, a factor to consider, especially knowing that some ingredients in mainline beers, such as hops, are often treated with pesticides. "By 2013, organic beer will need to use organic hops where they now can use a combination of organic and non-organic," Pleuss continues.

"I would suggest that the first priority in buying organic would be putting the extra money toward organic produce," she laughs.

Another new product, bottle-conditioned beer, has brewer's yeast added before the bottle is closed, supposedly augmenting the health benefits in yeast, such as B-complex vitamins, protein, chromium and other good "stuff." But the health value would depend on how much extra brewer's yeast is in the beer and how much is in the sediment on the bottom that would not be ingested, says Pleuss, whose favorite style of beer is a pilsner. She enjoys the occasional Miller MGD 64, with only sixty-four calories and 2.4 carbs. Pleuss prefers "the colder, the better."

While some researchers have said that beer can improve cholesterol metabolism and is a source of antioxidants, Pleuss still warns that beer or any alcohol actually increases the risk of cancer, especially of the breast, liver, rectum, throat, mouth and esophagus. As a last word regarding beer as part of one's health plan: "Don't start drinking if you currently don't drink," she advised.

Dr. Robert Gleeson, director of the Froedtert Hospital & the Medical College of Wisconsin Executive Health Program, agreed with much of what Pleuss says and emphasized, "I highly doubt that the addition of fruit to beer has any added health benefit." He goes on, "Sorry, but I cannot find what I accept as good science anything that separates the health benefits of beer from other alcohols."

When Gleeson needs such backgrounding and resources in his work, he often cites Dr. David J. Hanson, of the State University of New York at Potsdam, who has researched the subject of alcohol and drinking for more than forty years.

"Moderate drinkers tend to have better health and live longer than those who are either abstainers or heavy drinkers," said Hanson, citing studies done by Harvard, the University of London, the Cancer Research Center, the National Institute on Alcohol Abuse and other research in Italy, Canada, Spain, Australia, the United Kingdom, Denmark and China.

Hanson, more of a wine than beer drinker himself, along with enjoying an occasional gin and tonic, indicates that in addition to having fewer heart attacks and strokes, moderate consumers of beer, wine and distilled spirits are generally less likely to suffer strokes, diabetes, arthritis, enlarged prostates, dementia and several major cancers.

As Hanson explains, a standard drink is a twelve-ounce bottle or can of regular beer, a five-ounce glass of wine one and a half ounces of 80-proof distilled spirits (either straight or in a mixed drink). "The alcohol content of a standard drink of beer, dinner wine or distilled spirits is equivalent. To a breathalyzer, they are all the same," he said.

The health benefits associated with drinking in moderation are also similar for beer, wine and spirits. The primary factor associated with health and longevity appears to be the alcohol itself," Hanson said, echoing both Pleuss and Gleeson.

"The pattern of consumption makes the most difference. It's much better to consume a little on a daily basis, rather than infrequently, for maximum health benefits." In other words, saving up for a week's worth of alcohol for the weekend is "unhealthful, even dangerous and clearly to be avoided," Hanson concluded.

Looking over his long years of study on the subject, Hanson recalled a conference debating ten studies on which kind of alcohol might be better healthwise. Three cited wine, three cited beer, three cited distilled spirits and one was inconclusive. And then the conferees adjourned to the bar.

Among the positive aspects of alcohol, Hanson points out that it reduces coronary artery spasm in response to stress, increases coronary blood flow, reduces blood pressure and reduces blood insulin levels and increases estrogen levels.

Like other science and medical professionals, he urges moderation, rarely having more than one to three drinks per day. "Unfortunately, there really can be too much of a good thing," Hanson warned.[10]

Notes

If you are going to build a brewery in any city, it has to be Milwaukee, especially with its history.
— *Jim Sorenson, owner, Horny Goat Brewing Company*

CHAPTER 1

1. "Beginnings, Dates and Events."
2. "The Fur Trade Era: 1650s–1850s."
3. Brown, *Wines and Beers*, 184.
4. Reilly, "Hop Growing in Lisbon."
5. *Milwaukee Journal*, "Birth of Milwaukee's Brewing."
6. *Milwaukee Sentinel*, "The First Milwaukee Brewery."
7. Reilly, "A History of Milwaukee and Wisconsin Breweries."
8. "Brewing and Prohibition."

CHAPTER 2

1. Eastberg, *Captain Frederick Pabst Mansion*, 164.
2. Uihlein genealogy tables.
3. Anderson, *The Beer Book*, 182.
4. Wirth, *Chronik der Stadt Miltenberg.*
5. Paradis and Brumder, *German Milwaukee*, 35.

6. Ibid.

7. Bruce and Currey, *History of Milwaukee*, 694–97.

8. *August Krug, Last Will & Testament.*

9. "History of American Beer."

10. Uihlein genealogy tables.

11. Bruce, *History of Milwaukee*, 698.

12. "Sketches of Some of the Lost."

13. Bruce, *History of Milwaukee*, 696.

14. Reilly, "Joseph Schlitz Brewing Co."

15. Paradis and Brumder, *German Milwaukee*, 35–36.

16. "Joseph Schlitz Brewing Company History."

17. Milwaukee Ballet Company.

18. Wells, *Yesterday's Milwaukee*, 87; "Cinema Treasures: The Alhambra Theater."

19. Bruce, *History of Milwaukee*, 55, 697.

20. Yenne, *Great American Beers*, 151.

21. "Women's Christian Temperance Union."

22. Wells, *Yesterday's Milwaukee*, 91.

23. Kroll, *Badger Breweries*, 1.

24. Layden, "Naples Home That Sold for $40M."

25. Uihlein genealogy tables; *Milwaukee Sentinel*, "J.E. Uihlein, Sr., Dies."

26. Yenne, *Great American Beers*, 151.

27. Priest and Stewart, *Handbook of Brewing*, 558.

28. *Milwaukee Sentinel*, "J.E. Uihlein Sr."; *Milwaukee Journal* "Joseph E. Uihlein Sr. Dies."

29. Yenne, *Great American Beers*, 151.

30. Brumder, "Individual Summary."

31. Ingham, *Biographical Dictionary*, 1,484.

32. Reilly, *Joseph Schlitz Brewing Company.*

33. Cochran, *Pabst Brewing Company*, 338–40.

34. Hintz, *Afterglow*, 10.

35. Anderson and Olson, *Milwaukee*, 211.

36. Yenne, *Great American Beers*, 151.

37. Priest and Stewart, *Handbook of Brewing*, 560.

38. Yenne, *Great American Beers*, 154.

39. Ogle, *Ambitious Brew*, 239.

40. Ingham. *Biographical Dictionary*, 1,484.

41. "Pabst Revises Schlitz."

42. Ingham, *Biographical Dictionary*, 1,486.

43. "Milwaukee Beer History."

44. Ogle, *Ambitious Brew*, 247; "History and Advertising."

45. Gurda, *Making of Milwaukee*, 418; Ogle, *Ambitious Brew*, 248.

46. "The Great Circus Parade."

47. Anderson and Olson, *Milwaukee*, 156.

48. Reilly, "Joseph Schlitz Brewing Co."; interviews with Jack McKeithan, former Jos. Schlitz Brewing Co. president.

49. Bucurel, "Schlitz Beer Returns to Madison Liquor Stores"; Daykin, "Schlitz Again Being Brewed."

50. Daykin, "Pabst Brings Back the Schlitz 'Tall Boy' Can."

51. Eastberg, *Captain Frederick Pabst Mansion*, 37–38.

52. Burnley, *Millionaires and Kings of Enterprise*, 465; Cochrane, *Pabst Brewing Company*, 47.

53. *Milwaukee Journal*, "Marine Intelligence."

54. Cochrane, *Pabst Brewing Company*, 92; Paradis and Brumder. *German Milwaukee*, 30–31.

55. Zeldes, "Chicago Gave Pabst Its Blue Ribbon."

56. Eastberg, *Captain Frederick Pabst Mansion*, 45.

57. "The Pabst Mansion."

58. "History of the Pabst Theater."

59. *Milwaukee Sentinel*, "Congressman Lentz in Milwaukee."

60. Interview, John Eastberg, senior historian, Historic Pabst Mansion.

61. Eastberg, *Captain Frederick Pabst Mansion*, 42, 85; Weiner, *Taster's Guide to Beer*, 203.

62. "Probate Trial of the Estate of Captain Frederick Pabst."

63. Pririe, "Pabst Brewing Company."

64. Weiner, *Taster's Guide to Beer*, 204–05; Mulligan, "Pabst Brewing Company," 471–72.

65. "Pabst Brewing Co. Timeline"; Mittelman, *Brewing Battles*, 167.

66. Walker, "Marketing of No Marketing."

67. Gurda, *Making of Milwaukee*, 418; "Clock Ticking on Pabst Sale"; Horne, "New Owners Sought for Pabst"; "Paul Kalmanovitz, 81; Owned Pabst Brewing."

68. Lattman and Kesmodel, "Pabst's New Owner Built Fortune"; "Alert! Hipsters."

69. www.pabstbrewingco.com.

70. "The Pabst Mansion."

71. "The Brewery"; "Best Place Milwaukee."

72. Gurda, *Miller Time*, 4.

73. "Miller History"; John, *Miller Beer Barons*, 19–23.

74. Gurda, *Miller Time*, 23; John, *Miller Beer Barons*, 24–32.

75. Gurda, *Miller Time*, 23, 26.

76. "Miller Brewing History."

77. Ibid.

78. Ogle, *Ambitious Brew*, 242; "Miller Brewing History."

79. John, *Miller Beer Barons*, 392.

80. "Miller Brewing CEO Warren Dunn."

81. "Miller Brewing History"; Gurda, *Miller Time*, 166–69.

82. Janofsky, "A New Chief For Miller Brewing Co."; *Modern Brewery Age*, "John Bowlin Is New Miller CEO."

83. *Food Engineering*, "Miller Brewing Company"; Gurda, *Miller Time*, 170–71; John, *Miller Beer Barons*, 395–96

84. MillerCoors.

85. Apps, *Breweries of Wisconsin*, 99; "History of Blatz Brewing Company."

86. Apps, *Breweries of Wisconsin*, 99; "History of Blatz Brewing Company."

87. Mittelman, *Brewing Battles*, 153; "Schenley Industries."

88. "Schenley Industries."

89. "Blatz History"; "History of Blatz Brewing Company"; Anderson, *The Beer Book*, 183.

90. "Blatz Brewery Complex."

91. *History of Milwaukee, Wisconsin*, 1,476.

92. Gettelman, letter.

93. Rommel, "Grand Taste from the Past."

94. *Milwaukee Journal*, "Humble Butcher Paper Sketch Starts Industry."

95. *Milwaukee Sentinel*, "Miller Buys Gettelman; Price 'Over a Million.'"

CHAPTER 3

1. Daykin, "Sprecher Giving Brewery's Reins."

2. Decker, "Sprecher Forms New Brewing Venture."

3. Interviews, Randy Sprecher, president, Sprecher Brewing Company.

4. Daykin, "Can-Do Brewers."

5. Snyder, "Dorothy, This Isn't the Stork Club Anymore."

6. *Small Business Times*, "Gluten-free Beer Fuels Growth."

7. Sherman, "The Greener Side of Milwaukee."

8. Daykin, "Lakefront Now a Craft Brewery."

9. "History of the Lakefront Brewery"; Mallozzi, "Fans in a Froth for the Mug."

10. Hintz, "Brew Town Revival," 72–75.
11. "Lakefront Brewery"; interviews, Russ Klisch, co-owner, Lakefront Brewery.
12. www.waterstreetbrewery.com; interviews, George Bluvas, brewmaster; Tina Lukowitz, marketing director.
13. www.ale-house.com; interviews, Jim McCabe, president, Milwaukee Brewing Company; Sue Black, director of Milwaukee County Department of Parks, Recreation & Culture.
14. "Horny Goat Brewing Company"; interviews, Jim Sorenson, president, Horny Goat Brewing Company; Hintz, "Brew Town Revival."
15. *Shepherd Express*, "Boris & Doris on the Town"; www.bigbaybrewing.com; Hintz, "Brew Town Revival." Ibid.
16. "St. Francis Brewing Company"; interview, Sue DeGeorge, manager, St. Francis Brewery and Restaurant; Hintz, "Brew Town Revival."
17. "Stonefly Brewing Company"; interviews, Julia LaLoggia, co-owner, Stonefly Brewing Company; Hintz, "Brew Town Revival."

CHAPTER 4

1. Patti, "Wisconsin Whiskey."
2. "Antique Wisconsin Whiskey Flask Bottle Gallery"; "Wisconsin Whiskey Brands."
3. Cullen, "Milwaukee Downtown Brewing History Tour."
4. *History of Milwaukee, Wisconsin*, 1,474.
5. "J.P. Kissinger & Co."
6. "Wisconsin Whiskey Brands."
7. Lindsay, "Death of the Milwaukee Liquor Industry"; "Milwaukee Distilling."
8. *Cream City Courier*, "The Wm. Bergenthal Co."; Lindsay, "Death of the Milwaukee Liquor Industry"; www.slahs.org/brewery/liquor/industry_death.htm; Hintz, *Universal Foods*, 6–7.
9. Ibid.
10. *Clubmen of New York*, 843; *The Foundry* 37, no. 6 (February 1911), 282; "History of the Milwaukee Athletic Club."
11. Wells. *This Is Milwaukee*, 202–03.
12. Chuck Cowdery; Lipman, "S.C. Herbst"; Lipman, "Ghosts of Whiskies Past."
13. www.straightbourbon.com/forums/showthread.php?t=435.

14. "Sensient Technologies Corporation."

15. Hintz, " Sip Locally," 20–22.

16. "Great Lakes Distillery"; interviews, Guy Rehorst, Great Lakes Distillery.

17. Interview, David Turk, United States Marshals Service.

18. "Roaring Dan Rum"; Sandusky, "Great Lakes Piracy," 6; Bie, "The Life & Crimes of Dan Seavey"; Herrmann, "Lake Michigan's Very Own Pirate."

Chapter 5

1. Gurda, *Making of Milwaukee*, 64.

2. "Milwaukee Timeline."

3. Wells, *This Is Milwaukee*, 100.

4. *Milwaukee Sentinel*, "Saloons of Milwaukee."

5. *Milwaukee Journal*, "When Beer, Milwaukee Style."

6. "Biography for Spencer Tracy."

7. "History of the School Sisters of St. Francis."

8. Kertscher, "Per Person, Franklin Leads County."

9. Schumacher, *German Milwaukee*, 88, 98,103–105; Reilly, "A History of Milwaukee"; Wells, *This Is Milwaukee*, 109.

10. "Final Historic Designation Study Report."

11. *History of Milwaukee, Wisconsin*, 1,437; Widen, *Entertainment in Early Milwaukee*, 30.

12. "The Family History of Bernhard & Philomena Bittmann."

13. Opening program, Schlitz Palm Garden.

14. "Woodrow Wilson."

15. *Cleveland Socialist*, "Our Candidates: Emil Seidel."

16. "City Smart: Milwaukee"; "Beer Gardens."

17. *Milwaukee Journal*, "When Beer, Milwaukee Style, Was Introduced."

18. "Sheepshead"; Rosch, *A Field Guide to Sheepshead*.

19. Buck, *Pioneer History of Milwaukee*.

20. McCann, "Crazy Water Replaces Zur Krone."

21. "Mader's History."

22. "Karl Ratzsch's Restaurant."

23. "Bavarian Inn History."

24. *Shepherd Express*, "Milwaukee's Schwabenhof Keeps German Heritage Alive."

25. "Kegel's Inn."

26. Alioto, *Milwaukee's Brady Street Neighborhood*, 20.

27. Ibid., 93.

28. "Museum of Beer & Brewing."

29. *Milwaukee Sentinel*, "Breweries Purchasing Saloon Properties."

30. Ibid.

31. Hintz. *Afterglow: The Story of a Farm*. Ibid. p. 18.

32. "Milwaukee Beer History."

33. "Permanent Historic Designation Study Report," 2–5.

34. Tanzillo, "Club Garibaldi Remains a Corner Tap."

35. Alioto, *Milwaukee's Brady Street Neighborhood*, 18, 107.

36. Gauer, *Growing Up the Hard Way*, 40.

37. Ibid.

38. Ibid., 40–41, 154.

39. Ibid., 42.

40. Ibid.

41. Ibid., 52.

42. "Milwaukee Press Club History"; "The Safe House."

43. "Holler House, The Best Bars in America."

44. "The Holler House."

45. "Koz's History."

46. "Landmark Lanes History."

47. "Hooligan's Super Bar."

48. Hintz, "Close Wolski's," 55.

49. "Wolski's Cancels 2007 Pub Crawl."

50. "Fitzgibbons' Pub, Over 105 Yeas of Bitter Bartending."

51. Hintz, "Roman's Pub."

52. Wells, *This Is Milwaukee*, 72.

53. Hintz, *Irish Milwaukee*, 14; Archdiocese of Milwaukee Catholic Cemeteries.

54. Ziemba, "On the Ramble."

55. Hintz, *Irish Milwaukee*, 13; "*Lady Elgin* Passenger List."

56. *Irish American Post*, "*Lady Elgin* Sinking Told in New Play."

57. Witt, "Josie Nash RIP"; Hintz, *Irish Milwaukee*, 65.

58. Hintz, *Irish Milwaukee*, 72; Walker, "Last Call for Jim Hegarty's Pub."

59. Hintz, *Irish Milwaukee*, 72.

60. "County Clare"; *Irish American Post*, "New Locke's on Life."

61. Neville, "Hegarty's Irish Pub."

62. Hintz, *Irish Milwaukee*, 72.

63. Hintz, *Irish Milwaukee*, 72; Hintz, "Milwaukee's Irish Bars."

64. "Irish Cultural and Heritage Center."
65. Hintz, "Milwaukee's Irish Bars."

CHAPTER 6

1. *Milwaukee Sentinel*, "Enforcement Chief Speaks Out."
2. *Green Bay Press Gazette*, "Green Bay Badger Cradle of Temperance."
3. *Wisconsin Temperance Journal*.
4. Wheeler, *Chronicles of Milwaukee*, 106, 111.
5. Hintz, *Irish Milwaukee*, 8.
6. Gleeson, "Parade History."
7. Ranney, "Demon Rum and Sunday Lager."
8. "Brewing and Prohibition"; Kasparek, Malone and Schock, *Wisconsin History Highlights*.
9. Merz, *Dry Decade*, 14–15.
10. Asbury, *Great Illusion*, 136.
11. United States Constitution.
12. Congressional Record, 1919.
13. "Subtitle of the Act," http://www.druglibrary.org/schaffer/Library/studies/wick/wick1.html.
14. Hintz, *Afterglow*, 14; Eighteenth Amendment.
13. National Prohibition Act (Volstead Act) and related Prohibition documents.
14. Gurda, *Making of Milwaukee*, 238.
15. Crepeau, "Prohibition in Milwaukee"; Lucker, "Politics of Prohibition."
16. *Milwaukee Telegram*, "Quin and Neacy."
17. Hintz, *Afterglow*, 15; "The Eline Chocolate Factory."
18. *Milwaukee Sentinel*, "Drink Victim Hospitalized."
19. *Milwaukee Sentinel*, "Agent Needs Rescue from Mob."
20. *Milwaukee Sentinel*, "Police Raids Sweep Milwaukee."
21. *Milwaukee Sentinel*, "Klan Goes After Rum."
22. *Milwaukee Sentinel*, "Arrests."
23. Office of the Sheriff, Milwaukee County, *1835–2000, Wisconsin*, 58; Wells, *Yesterday's Milwaukee*, 105.
24. Hoan, letter; Lucker, "Politics of Prohibition," 77.
25. *Milwaukee Sentinel* and *Milwaukee Journal*, 1920–35.
26. *Milwaukee Sentinel*, "Violators Arraigned."
27. *Sunday Sentinel and Telegram*, "Alcohol Statistics."

28. "John Blaine."
29. Hintz, *Farewell, John Barleycorn*, 79.
30. Gurda, *Making of Milwaukee*, 297; photograph, Milwaukee County Historical Society.
31. Twenty-first Amendment.

CHAPTER 7

1. Mickelsen, "Famous Gardens and Wein Stuben."
2. Herzog, "Beer Hops Out of the Glass."
3. Percy, "Chef Speak: Tom Peschong," 112.
4. Hintz, "Top Chef," 18.
5. Percy, "Chef Speak: Thi Cao," 62.
6. "Biography: Sanford D'Amato."
7. "Grilling with Beer Contest—2010."
8. "History of The Falk Brewing Company"; *Daily Northwestern*, "Militia Out"; *Daily Northwestern*, "Bloodshed, Several Men Killed"; Gurda, *Making of Milwaukee*, 150–56.
9. Gurda, *Miller Time*, 64.
10. Hintz, "Beer With Benefits," 70–71.

Bibliography

BOOKS

Alioto, Frank D. *Images of America: Milwaukee's Brady Street Neighborhood*. Charleston, SC: Arcadia Publishing, 2008.

Anderson, Will. *The Beer Book*. Princeton, NJ: Pyne Press, 1973.

Andreas. A.T., ed. *History of Milwaukee, Wisconsin*. Chicago: Western Historical Company, 1881.

Apps, Jerry. *Breweries of Wisconsin*. Madison: University of Wisconsin Press, 1992.

Asbury, Herbert. *The Great Illusion: An Informal History of Prohibition*. Garden City, NJ: Doubleday, 1950.

Brown, Sanborn. *Wines and Beers of Old New England: A How-to-Dop-It History*. Lebanon, NH: University Press of New England, 1998.

Bruce, William George, and Josiah Seymour Currey. *The History of Milwaukee, City and County*. Vol. 3. Chicago: S.J. Clarke Publishing Co., 1922.

Burnley, James. *Millionaires and Kings of Enterprise: The Marvelous Careers of Some Americans Who by Pluck, Foresight, and Engery Have Made Themselves Masters in the Fields of Industry and Finance*. London: Harmsworth Brothers, 1901.

Clubmen of New York. 4th ed. New York: W.S. Rossiter, 1901.

Cochrane, Thomas. *The Pabst Brewing Company, The History of an American Business*. New York: New York University Press, 1948. Reprint, Cleveland, OH: Beerbooks, 2006.

A Company Transformed: Sensient Technologies Corporation at 125 Years. Milwaukee, WI: Sensient Technologies, 2007.

Eastberg, John. *The Captain Frederick Pabst Mansion: An Illustrated History*. Milwaukee, WI: Captain Frederick Pabst Mansion, Inc., 2009.

Gauer, Harold. *The History, Vol. 1: Growing Up the Hard Way in the 1930s*. Milwaukee, WI: Precision Process/Urge Press, 1989.

Gettelman, Nancy Moore. *A History of A. Gettelman Brewing Company*. Milwaukee, WI: Procrustes Press, 1995.

Gurda, John. *Making of Milwaukee*. Milwaukee, WI: Milwaukee Historical Society, 1999.

———. *Miller Time*. Milwaukee, WI: Miller Brewing Company, 2006.

Hintz, Martin. *Afterglow: The Story of a Farm*. Milwaukee, WI: Glenoble Publishing, 2010.

———. *Farewell John Barleycorn*. Minneapolis, MN: Lerner Publishing, 1996.

———. *Images of America: Irish Milwaukee*. Charleston, SC: Arcadia Publishing, 2003.

———. *Universal Foods: First 100 Years*. Milwaukee, WI: Universal Foods, 1982.

Ingham, John. *Biographical Dictionary of American Business Leaders*. Westport, CT: Greenwood Publishing Group, 1983.

John, Tim. *The Miller Beer Barons*. Oregon, WI: Badger Books, Inc., 2005.

Jon, Bobbie Malone, and Erica Schock. *Wisconsin History Highlights: Delving into the Past*. Madison: Wisconsin Historical Society Press, 2004.

Korman, Gerd. *Industrialization, Immigrants and Americanizers: The View from Milwaukee, 1866–1921*. Madison: State Historical Society of Wisconsin, 1967.

Merz, Charles. *The Dry Decade*. Garden City, NJ: Doubleday, 1932.

Mittelman, Amy. *Brewing Battles: A History of American Beer*. New York: Algora Publishing, 2007.

Mulligan, William, Jr. "Pabst Brewing Company." In *Alcohol and Temperance in Modern History: A Global Encyclopedia*. 2 vols. Santa Barbara, CA: ABC-CLIO, 2003.

Office of the Sheriff, Milwaukee County. *1835–2000, Wisconsin*. Milwaukee County, 2000.

———. *Millennium History Book*. Paducah, KY: Turner Publishing Co., 2000.

Ogle, Maureen. *Ambitious Brew: The Story of American Beer*. New York: Harcourt Publishing, 2006.

Paradis, Trudy Knauss, and E.J. Brumder. *German Milwaukee: Its History, Its Recipes*. St. Louis: G. Bradley Publishing, 2006.

Parker, Robert. *Brimestone*. New York: G.P. Putnam's Sons, 2009.

Priest, Fergus G., and Graham G. Stewart, ed. *Handbook of Brewing*. Boca Raton, FL: CRC Press/Taylor & Francis Group, 2007.

Rosch. Erica M. *A Field Guide to Sheepshead*. Oregon, WI: Badger Books, 2001.

Schumacher, Jennifer Watson, ed. *Images of America: German Milwaukee*. Charleston: Arcadia Publishing, 2009.

Tremblay, Victor J., and Carol Horton Tremblay. *The U.S. Brewing Industry: Data and Economic Analysis*. Cambridge: Massachusetts Institute of Technology, 2005.

Weiner, Michael A. *The Taster's Guide to Beer*. New York: Macmillan Publishing Co., 1977.

Wells, Robert W. *This Is Milwaukee*. Garden City, NY: Doubleday & Co., 1970.

————. *Yesterday's Milwaukee*. Miami, FL: E.A. Seemann Publishing, 1976.

Wheeler, A.C. *Chronicles of Milwaukee*. Milwaukee, WI: Jermain & Brightman Publishers, 1861.

Widen, Larry. *Entertainment in Early Milwaukee*. Charleston, SC: Arcadia Publishing, 2007.

Wirth, Michael Josef. *Chronik der Stadt Miltenberg, Miltenberg.* 1890. Reprint, Neustadt/ Aisch, 1987.

Yenne, William, *Great American Beers*. St. Paul, MN: MBI Publishing Co., 2003.

INTERVIEWS, CONTACTS, ASSISTS

Sue Black, director of Milwaukee County Department of Parks, Recreation & Culture

George Bluvas, brewmaster, Water Street Brewery

Mike Brenner, Brenner Brewing Co.

E.J. Brumder, genealogist/historian

Thi Cao, executive chef, Café Calatrava, Milwaukee Art Museum

Darlene Carlson, Andrew Gregg, University of Wisconsin–Milwaukee

Sanford D'Amato, Sanford Restaurant

Sister Corrine Dias, Sister Mary Ann Eichenseer, archivists, School Sisters of St. Francis

Sue DeGeorge, manager, St. Francis Brewery and Restaurant

John Eastberg, senior historian, Historic Pabst Mansion

Elisabeth Engel, curator of collections, Waukesha County Historical Society and Museum

Jeff Garwood, owner, Big Bay Brewing Company

Dr. Robert Gleeson, director, Froedtert Hospital & the Medical College of Wisconsin Executive Health Program

Julian Green, media relations director, Miller/Coors

Dr. David J. Hanson, State University of New York at Potsdam

David Herrewig, archivist, Miller/Coors

Tim John, great-grandson of Frederick Miller, founder of Miller Brewing

Russ Klisch, co-owner, Lakefront Brewery

Julia LaLoggia, co-owner, Stonefly Brewing Company

Tina Lukowitz, marketing director, Water Street Brewing

Doris Maki, Milwaukee County Department of Parks, Recreation & Culture

Peter Marino, Dig Communications

Jim McCabe, president, Milwaukee Brewing Company/Milwaukee Ale House

Jack McKeithan, former president, Jos. Schlitz Brewing Co.

Mary Niland, manager, Maders Restaurant

Joseph Pabst, great-great-grandson of Captain Frederick Pabst, founder
    of Pabst Brewing

Tom Peschong, executive chef, Riversite Restaurant

Jeff (Whispering Jeff) Platt, publisher, *Suds, Wine & Spirits*

Joan Pleuss, bionutrition director for the Translational Research Unit at the
    Medical College of Wisconsin

Guy Rehorst, president, Great Lakes Distillery

Mike Roman, owner, Roman's Tavern

Adam Siegel, executive chef, Bartolotta Restaurant Group

Jim Sorenson, co-owner, Horney Goat Hideaway & Brewery

Anne Sprecher, vice-president, Sprecher Brewing Company

Randy Sprecher, president, Sprecher Brewing Company

John Steinmiller, media relations, MillerCoors-Milwaukee

David Turk, historian, United States Marshals Service

David Uihlein Jr., Lynde Uihlein, grandchildren of Joseph Uihlein, president
    Jos. Schlitz Brewing

David Uihlein Sr., son of Joseph Uihlein, president Jos. Schlitz Brewing

Tim Wright, Sprecher Brewing Company

OTHER

Anti-Saloon League Year Book, 1919.

City of Milwaukee. "Final Historic Designation Study Report: Trinity
    Lutheran Church Complex." August 7, 2002.

———."Permanent Historic Designation Study Report Former Schlitz
    Tavern/Coventry Inn, 2501 West Greenfield Avenue." December 2009.

Communications Department, Corporate Affairs Division, Miller Brewing Co. *Miller History*. Pamphlet, Fall 1991.

Congressional Record, 1919. Vol. 65, pp. 1944, 3005, 4908, 7610–7611, 7633–7634.

Crepeau, Richard C. "Prohibition in Milwaukee." Master's thesis, Marquette University, July 1967.

Cullen, Kevin. Milwaukee Downtown Brewing History Tour, April 21, 2010.

Gettelman, Adam, to Milwaukee Fire Chief Henry Lippert, letter. November 3, 1877.

The Great Pabst Brewery Milwaukee. Pamphlet. Milwaukee, WI: Pabst Brewing Company, 1907.

Krug, August. *Last Will & Testament, May 19, 1856*. Complied by Mike Reilly. Sussex-Lisbon Area Historical Society.

Lipinski, Eileen, Legislative Library manager. Legislative Reference Bureau, City of Milwaukee, January 18, 2011.

Lucker, Jeffrey. "The Politics of Prohibition in Wisconsin, 1917–1933." Master's thesis, University of Wisconsin, 1968.

Miller Brewing Company v. Brewery Workers Local Union No. 9, AFL-CIO, Defendant-Appellee; No. 83-2048; United States Court of Appeals, Seventh Circuit. Argued April 11, 1984; decided June 25, 1984. 739 F.2d 1159 116 L.R.R.M. (BNA) 3130, 101 Lab.Cas. P 11,091.

National Distilling/Red Star Yeast. Company records, 1880s-current. Plus interviews with corporate officers.

National Prohibition Act (Volstead Act) and related Prohibition documents. www.archives.gov/education/lessons/volstead-act.

Opening program. Schlitz Palm Garden, 1896.

Pabst Brewing Company. "Pabst Brewing Co. Timeline."

"Probate Trial of the Estate of Captain Frederick Pabst, Milwaukee County." February 3, 1903.

Uihlein genealogy tables. Compiled by E.J. Brumder.

Wisconsin Temperance Journal 1, no. 1 (April 1840).

PERIODICALS

Beverage World. "Clock Ticking on Pabst Sale." September 9, 2008.

Bucurel, Dave. "Schlitz Beer Returns to Madison Liquor Stores." *Badger Herald*, September 9, 2008.

Cream City Courier. "The Wm. Bergenthal Co., Milwaukee, Wisconsin." 1900.

Daily Northwestern. "Bloodshed, Several Men Killed in Milwaukee." May 5, 1886.

———. "Militia Out, Fighting Going on in Milwaukee Today." May 4, 1886.

Daykin, Tom, "Can-Do Brewers," *Milwaukee Journal-Sentinel*, May 17, 2011.

———. "Lakefront Now a Craft Brewery." *Milwaukee Journal Sentinel*, November 24, 2010.

———. "Pabst Brings Back the Schlitz 'Tall Bo' Can." *Milwaukee Journal Sentinel*, March 2, 2010.

———. "Schlitz Again Being Brewed, Bottled in Milwaukee." *Milwaukee Journal-Sentinel*, January 29, 2009.

———. "Sprecher Giving Brewery's Reins to Manager Hamilton." *Milwaukee Journal Sentinel*, February 27, 2010.

Food Engineering. "Miller Brewing Company Names Norman Adami President." May 1, 2003.

Green Bay Press Gazette. "Green Bay Badger Cradle of Temperance Movement." May 25, 1921.

Herrmann, Andrew. "Lake Michigan's Very Own Pirate; 'Low-life Scum' Fascinated City Nearly 100 Years Ago." *Chicago Sun-Times*, June 11, 2007.

Herzog, Karen. "Beer Hops Out of the Glass and into the Deep-Fryer." *Milwaukee Journal-Sentinel*, October 1, 2010.

Hintz, Martin. "Beer Lovers Paradise." *M Magazine*, March 2011.

———. "Beer With Benefits." *M Magazine*, March 2011.

———. "Brew Town Revival." *M Magazine*, March 2011.

———. "Milwaukee's Irish Bars." *M Magazine*, March 2011.

———. "Old Distillery Reborn in Kilbeggan…Slainté." *Irish American Post* 1, no. 11 (April 2001).

———. "Roman's Pub." *M Magazine*, March 2011.

———. "Sip Locally." *Wisconsin Trails*, February, 2009, pp. 20-22.

———. "Top Chef," *M Magazine*, December 2008.

Huffington Post. "Alert! Hipsters: Pabst Beer Sold to Food Kingpin C. Dean Metropoulos." May 26, 2010.

Janofsky, Michael. "A New Chief For Miller Brewing Co. *New York Times*, August 24, 1993.

Kertscher, Tom. "Per Person, Franklin Leads County in Liquor Licenses." *Milwaukee Journal-Sentinel*, December 31, 2009.

"*Lady Elgin* Sinking Told in New Play: 'A Rising Wind.'" *Irish American Post* 11, no. 1 (Winter 2010–2011).

Lattman, Peter, and David Kesmodel. "Pabst's New Owner Built Fortune on Old Brands." *Wall Street Journal*, May 26, 2010.

Mallozzi, Vincent. "Fans in a Froth for the Mug in Which Bernie Brewer Bathed." *New York Times*, September 23, 2007.

Mickelsen, Gunnar. "Famous Gardens and Wein Stuben Gave City Its Charm in the Early Days." *Milwaukee Sentinel*, February 21, 1932.

Milwaukee Journal. "Humble Butcher Paper Sketch Starts Industry." July 2, 1933.

———. "Joseph E. Uihlein Sr., Retired Brewer, Dies." January 8, 1968.

———. "Marine Intelligence." August 26, 1891.

———. "Schlitz Garden Enters History." March 6, 1921.

———. "When Beer, Milwaukee Style, Was Introduced to New York." May 30, 1930.

Milwaukee Sentinel. "Agent Needs Rescue from Mob." May 31, 1920.

———. "Arrests." May 9, 11, 21 and July 1, 2, 1921.

———. "Birth of Milwaukee's Brewing Industry is Interesting Story." March 19, 1916.

———. "Breweries Purchasing Saloon Properties." April 26, 1885.

———. "Congressman Lentz in Milwaukee." November 25, 1899.

———. "Drink Victim Hospitalized." January 19, 1920.

———. "Enforcement Chief Speaks Out." December 21.

———. "The First Milwaukee Brewery." November 29, 1869.

———. "Fresh Beer." July 29, 1879.

———. "J.E. Uihlein, Sr., Dies at Age 92." January 8, 1968.

———. "Klan Goes After Rum." July 14, 1922.

———. "Miller Buys Gettelman; Price 'Over a Million." January 15, 1961.

———. "Police Raids Net Plenty of Stash." April 3, 1922.

———. "Saloons of Milwaukee." August 2, 1873.

———. "Violators Arraigned." March 18, 1927.

Milwaukee Telegram. "Quin and Neacy, Pioneers Here Flay Dry Laws." January 15, 1922.

Modern Brewery Age. "John Bowlin Is New Miller CEO." April 19, 1999.

Neville, Mike. "Hegarty's Irish Pub: And then the Archbishop Walks In." *Irish American Post* 8, no. 2 (Summer 2008).

"New Locke's on Life; Old Distillery Reborn in Kilbeggan...Slainté." *Irish American Post* 1, no. 11 (April 2001).

New York Times. "Paul Kalmanovitz, 81; Owned Pabst Brewing." Obituary, January 20, 1987.

"Our Candidates: Emil Seidel." *Cleveland Socialist* 48 (September 21, 1912).

Percy, Pam. "Chef Speak: Thi Cao." *M Magazine*, July 2010.

———. "Chef Speak: Tom Peschong." *M Magazine*, September 2008.

Shepherd Express. "Boris & Doris on the Town." February 10, 2011.

———. "Milwaukee's Schwabenhof Keeps German Heritage Alive." April 6, 2010.

Small Business Times. "Gluten-free Beer Fuels Growth for Lakefront Brewery." January 26, 2007.

Stevens Point Journal. "A Farmer's Wife." September 30, 1876.

Sunday Sentinel and Telegram. "Alcohol Statistics." January 20, 1929.

Walker, Rob. "The Marketing of No Marketing." *New York Times*, June 22, 2003.

Witt, Brian. "Josie Nash RIP, 'Goodbye, Luv, You're Going Home.'" *Irish American Post* (September 2001).

Zeldes, Leah A. "Chicago Gave Pabst Its Blue Ribbon—and a Tax Break." *Dining Chicago*, August 10, 2009.

Ziemba, Meaghan. "On the Ramble: During a Milwaukee Pub Crawl, Multiply the Craic." *Irish American Post* 8, no. 1 (Winter–Spring 2008).

WEBSITES

"Antique Wisconsin Whiskey Flask Bottle Gallery." http://www.mrbottles.com/galleryWhiskeyFlasks.asp.

"Bavarian Inn History." www.bavarianinnmilw.com.

"Beer from Thuringia." www.ratebeer.com/state/thuringia/126.

"Beer Gardens." http://www.answers.com/topic/beer-garden.

"Beginnings, Dates and Events." *History of Milwaukee City and County*. Chapter 16. 1890. www.hellomilwaukee.com/bookfiles/chap16_beginnings_dates_events1.pdf.

"Best Bars." http://www.esquire.com/bestbars/bb-HollerHouse.

"Best Place Milwaukee." www.bestplacemilwaukee.com.

Bie, Michael. "The Life & Crimes of Dan Seavey." ClassicWisconsin.com. http://www.classicwisconsin.com/features/ourpirate.htm, 2009.

"Big Bay Brewing Company." www.bigbaybrewing.com.

"Biography: Sanford D'Amato." www.sanfordrestaurant.com/sanford-restaurant-Sanford-Damato.htm.

"Biography for Spencer Tracy." Internet Movie Database. www.imdb.com/name/nm0000075/bio.

"Blatz Brewery Complex." www.landmarkhunter.com/179865-blatz-brewery-complex.

"Blatz History." www.angelfire.com/rant/punkmoore/Blatz/history.html.

"The Brewery." www.thebrewerymke.com.

"Brewing and Prohibition." Wisconsin Historical Society. www.wisconsinhistory.org.

Buck, James. *Pioneer History of Milwaukee*. Vol. 4. Milwaukee News Co., 1896. www.archive.org/stream/.../pioneerhistoryof04buck_djvu.txt.

"Cinema Treasures: The Alhambra Theater." cinematreasures.org/theater/2529.

"Craft Brewer Defined." Brewers Association, www.brewersassociation.org.

Decker, Eric. "Sprecher Forms New Brewing Venture." BizTimes.com. http://www.biztimes.com/news/2010/2/19/sprecher-forms-new-brewing-venture.

Eighteenth Amendment." www2.potsdam.edu/hansondj/.../The-Eighteenth-Amendment.htm.

"The Eline Chocolate Factory." oldmilwaukee.net/forum/viewtopic.php?f=18&t=409&si.

"The Family History of Bernhard & Philomena Bittmann." www.freepages.genealogy.rootsweb.ancestry.com/~bittman/bbitt.htm.

"Fitzgibbons' Pub, Over 105 Years of Bitter Bartending." www.fitzgibbonspub.com.

"The Fur Trade Era: 1650s–1850s." Wisconsin Historical Society. www.wisconsinhistory.org/topics/shorthistory/furtrade.asp.

Gleeson, John, ed. "Parade History." http://saintpatricksparade.org/history.php.

"Great Lakes Distillery." www.greatlakesdistillery.com.

"Grilling with Beer Contest—2010." www.sprecherbrewery.com/state-fair-recipes-2010.php.

"History and Advertising." Schlitz Brewing Co., www.pabstbrewingco.com.

"History of American Beer." http://beeradvocate.com/beer/101/history_american_beer.

"History of Blatz Brewing Company." www.blatzbeer.com.

"A History of Craft Brewing," www.brewersassociation.org.

"History of The Falk Brewing Company (1856–1892)." www.WisconsinBreweriana.com.

"History of the Lakefront Brewery." www.lakefrontbrewery.com/history.html.

"History of the Milwaukee Athletic Club." www.macwi.org.

"History of the Pabst Theater." www.pabsttheater.org.

"History of the School Sisters of St. Francis." www.sssf.org.

"The Holler House." en.wikipedia.org/wiki/Holler_House.

"Holler House, The Best Bars in America." www.esquire.com/bestbars/bb-HollerHouse.

"Hooligan's Super Bar." www.hooliganssuperbar.com.

Horne, Michael. "New Owners Sought for Pabst, Nov. 2, 2009." www.milwaukeeworld.com.

"Horny Goat Brewing Company." www.hornygoatbrewing.com.

"Irish Cultural and Heritage Center." www.irish-american.org.

"Joseph Schlitz Brewing Company History." http://www.antiqible.com/schlitz/history3.htm.

"J.P. Kissinger & Co." www.pre-pro.com/midacore/view_vendor.php?vid=MKE11391.

"Karl Ratzch's Restaurant." www.karlratzsch.com/history.htm.

"Kegel's Inn." www.kegelsinn.com.

"*Lady Elgin* Passenger List." www.ship-wrecks.net/shipwreck/projects/elgin/passengers.html.

"Lakefront Brewery History." www.lakefrontbrewery.com/history.html.

"Landmark Lanes History." www.landmarklanes.com/history.

Lindsay, John. "Death of the Milwaukee Liquor Industry." Sussex-Lisbon Area Historical Society. www.slahs.org/brewery/liquor/industry_death.htm.

Lipman, John F. "Ghosts of Whiskies Past: The Louisville Distilleries." *American Whiskey*. www.ellenjaye.com/ghosts2.htm.

"Mader's History." www.madersrestaurant.com.

McAlpine, Linda. "Memories of Prohibition in Our Area." GM Today. http://www.gmtoday.com/news/local_stories/2008/Nov_08/11262008_05.asp.

McCann, Kathleen. "Crazy Water Replaces Zur Krone With Fine Casual Dining." onmilwaukee.com.

Miller Brewing CEO Warren Dunn Named Beer Institute Chairman, PR Newswire, May 6, 1992. www.highbeam.com/doc/1G1-12212987.htm.

"Miller Brewing Company." www.fundinguniverse.com.

"Miller Brewing History." www.fundinguniverse.com/.../Miller-Brewing-Company-Company-History.html.

"MillerCoors." www.millercoors.com/who-we-are.

"Milwaukee Ballet History." http://www.milwaukeeballet.org/about-us/history.

"Milwaukee Beer History." Museum of Beer & Brewing, August 7, 2007. www.sudswineandspirits.com/milwaukeehistorytour.htm.

"Milwaukee Distilling." www.slahs.org/brewery/liquor/industry_death.htm.

"Milwaukee Press Club History." www.milwaukeepressclub.org.

"Milwaukee Timeline." Milwaukee County Historical Society. www.milwaukeehistory.net/milwaukee_timeline/1800s.html.

"Museum of Beer & Brewing: From Grain to Glass." August 7, 2007. www.sudswineandspirits.com/milwaukeehistorytour.htm.

Olson, Michael. "Melo's Minis." www.slahs.org/brewery/liquor/industry_death.htm. "Osthoff Resort History," http://www.osthoff.com.

"Our Namesake." Karl M. Strauss Brewing Company. www.karlstrauss.com.

"Pabst Brewing Company." www.pabstbrewingco.com

"The Pabst Mansion." www.pabstmansion.com

"Pabst Revises Schlitz." www.probrewer.com/bulletin/showthread.php?t=11581.

"Parade History." www.saintpatricksparade.org/history.php.

Patti, Emily. "Wisconsin Whiskey." ExpressMilwaukee.com. www.expressmilwaukee.com/article-11992-wisconsin-whiskey.html.

Pririe, Bob. "Pabst Brewing Company." *American Breweriana Journal*, January–February, 1994. www.pabst.nl/pabstbreweriana2.htm.

Ranney, Joseph A. "Demon Rum and Sunday Lager: The Temperance Movement in Wisconsin." *History of the Court System.* www.wicourts.gov.

Reilly, Michael. "A History of Milwaukee and Wisconsin Breweries." Sussex-Lisbon Area Historical Society. www.slahs.org/brewery/breweries.htm.

———. "Hop Growing in Lisbon, Washington County and Wisconsin." Sussex-Lisbon Area Historical Society. www.slahs.org/history/local/business/hops.htm.

———. "Joseph Schlitz Brewing Co.: A Chronological History." Sussex, Wisconsin: Sussex-Lisbon Area Historical Society. www.slahs.org/schlitz/history6.htm.

———. "Joseph Schlitz Brewing Co.: A Chronological History, 1969-1982." Sussex, Wis.: Sussex-Lisbon Area Historical Society. www.slahs.org/schlitz/history6.htm.

"Relations Between the Indians and the French." *Indian Country Wisconsin.* www.mpm.edu/wirp/ICW-145.html.

"Roaring Dan Rum." www.greatlakesdistillery.com/rum.htm.

Rommel, Rick. "Grand Taste from the Past." *Milwaukee Journal Sentinel*, September 5, 2007. www.jsonline.com/story/index.aspx?id=658060.

Sandusky, Trent. "Great Lakes Piracy: Pirates Thrived on the Great Lakes Long After Their Golden Age." http://www.associatedcontent.com/article/593863/great_lakes_piracy_pirates_thrived_pg3.html?cat=37.

"Schenley Industries." www.bottlebooks.com/American%20Medicinal%20Spirits%20Company/schenley.htm.

———. www.money.cnn.com/magazines/fortune/fortune500_archive/snapshots/1955/3515.html.

"Sensient Technologies Corporation." *Fundinguniverse*. www.fundinguniverse.com/company-histories.

Sherman, Jeannine. "The Greener Side of Milwaukee." *This Is Why I Come to Milwaukee*. www.visitmilwaukee.org/media.

Snyder, Molly. "Dorothy, This Isn't the Stork Club Anymore." onmilwaukee.com.

"St. Francis Brewery." www.stfrancisbrewery.com.

Straightbourbon.com. www.straightbourbon.com/forums/showthread.php?t=435.

Tanzillo, Bobby. "Club Garibaldi Remains a Corner Tap With City-Wide Appeal." onmilwaukee.com.

Walker, Don. "Last Call for Jim Hegarty's Pub: Generations of Marquette Students Found Friends at Tavern." www.jsonline.com.

Wikipedia. "Sheepshead." http://en.wikipedia.org/wiki/Sheepshead.

"Wisconsin Whiskey Brands." www.mrbottles.com/files/whiskeybrands.pdf.

"Wolski's Cancels 2007 Pub Crawl." http://wolskis.com/pubcrawl.htm.

"Woodrow Wilson." www.woodrowwilsonhouse.org/index.asp?section=timeline&file=timelinesearch_list&searchtype=date&month=&day=&year=1912&.

Zutz, John. "Welcome to Milwaukee: 35th Anniversary Opening Remarks." *Veteran*, Fall 2002. Vietnam Veterans Against the War. http://www.vvaw.org/veteran/article/?id=25.

Index

About the Author

Martin Hintz, author of *Forgotten Tales of Wisconsin* (The History Press, 2010), has written approximately one hundred books for Lerner, Capstone, Arcadia, Scholastic, Globe Pequot, Franklin Watts, Voyageur, Trails, Big Earth and others on various topics. These include: *Celebrate the Legend: 25 Years of Milwaukee Irish Fest* (Milwaukee Irish Fest, 2005*); Got Murder? The Shocking Story of Wisconsin's Notorious Killers* (Trails Publishing, 2007); coauthor, *Wisconsin Cheese: A Cookbook and Guide to the Cheeses of Wisconsin* (Globe Pequot, 2008); and *Off the Beaten Path: Wisconsin* (Globe Pequot Press, 1989, with subsequent reprints).

Articles published in major newspapers and consumer and trade periodicals include those in the *Chicago Tribune*, the *New York Post*, the *Chicago Sun Times*, *National Geographic World*, *Irish Music Magazine*, *Where to Retire Magazine*, *American Heritage*, *Interval*, *American Archaeology*, the *St. Petersburg Times*, the *Wisconsin Academy Review*, *Billboard*, *Amusement Business*, *Midwest Express Magazine*, the *Belfast News*, *City Lifestyle*, *Northshore Lifestyle*, the *Dodge Van Magazine; Jewish Heartland*, *Travel Holiday*, *Corporate Report Wisconsin*, *GolfWeek*, *Milwaukee Magazine*, *Shepherd Express*, the *Daily Herald*, the *Jewish Chronicle*, the *Writer*, *Midwest Living*, *MotorHome*, *Meetings California*, *Dig*, *Michigan Living*, *Home & Away*, *M Magazine*, *Group Travel Leader*, *Bus Tour Magazine* and numerous others.

Visit us at
www.historypress.net
....
This title is also available as an e-book